# System Busters

# How to Stop Them in Your Business

. . .eliminate bottlenecks, clean up messes, and make your
business run like a super-clean, well-oiled machine—
every single day, from now until the end of time—
whether you are there or not!

## PHILIP PAUL BEYER

Ebiz Products LLC • Nashville, Tennessee

Published by
Ebiz Products LLC
1855 Air Lane Drive
Nashville, TN 37210

info@ebizproducts.com

Cover concept by Philip and Susan Beyer


The Library of Congress Cataloging-in-Publication Data Applied For

Philip Paul Beyer, 1949
System Busters: How to Stop Them in Your Business
Philip Paul Beyer.—1st ed.
p.     cm
ISBN   978-0-9764822-3-9
1. Business  I. Title
2007

All scripture references
New King James Version © 1982 Thomas Nelson

Contributing Editors: Michael Christopher
and Susan Meredith Beyer


Printed in the United States of America
3  5  7  9  8  6  4  2
For information regarding special discounts for bulk sales
please contact the publisher at
info@ebizproducts.com

# DEDICATION

TO MY WIFE SUSAN MEREDITH BEYER—for her love, patience and encouragement always. Her input and editing skills were invaluable as I wrote this book.

TO MY LATE FATHER HENRY T. BEYER, JR.—a pastor and evangelist for fifty years—who taught me how to manage as I watched him stretch the small salary he made as a pastor that somehow allowed him to support a wife and eight children. My father introduced me to the number one Book on my list of preferred reading. He also introduced me to the Author of that Book.

TO MY MOTHER ARMELLIA STRIMEL BEYER—who not only taught, but demonstrated to me the value of hard work, stewardship and serving others.

TO MY THREE SONS PAUL, BARTON AND BRANDON—Paul was our first paid employee when we started our business in 1988, and he has been a witness to every mountain and valley along the way. I pray that all my sons will continue to build upon what we have accomplished here, that they might realize their own dreams.

TO GREG FAST AND MIKE SCHATZ OF GSF MEDIA—for their counsel that challenged me to take this book to another level.

TO MICHAEL CHRISTOPHER AND LISA WYSOCKY—whose editing and proofreading skills have taught me much about writing style.

FINALLY, TO EVERY ONE OF YOU WHO HOPE TO OWN A SUCCESSFUL BUSINESS—may this simple book plant a seed that will help you reap a harvest beyond anything you ever dreamed or imagined.

*Unless the Lord builds the house, they labor in vain who build it.*
King David

READ ON!

WITH OUR DEEPEST APPRECIATION

AND

IN MEMORY OF
# ROGER DICKESON*
(1921 - 2006)

IN THE SUMMER OF 2005, it was my great pleasure to finally get to talk with Mr. Roger Dickeson, after many years of reading his columns in the *Printing Impressions* magazine. I used to cut out many of his articles and save them. I can't tell you how much knowledge I gleaned from his wisdom over the years. At the time of our conversation, I had no idea that he was into his eighties—he seemed so vibrant and still excited about his industry. He was so curious about what we were doing with my book, *System Buster*, and with our *System100* software. In fact, I gave him an online demonstration, during which, he drilled me with question after question.

On two other occasions, he emailed me a long list of questions to answer—no doubt to make sure we had answers that would be beneficial to the people he had been helping for years. He loved the printing industry, and his heart was to ensure its prosperity by finding tools or ideas that would help it improve.

It was a great surprise, and one of the highlights of my life, to hear that Mr. Dickeson was going to do an article on our work in the October, 2005 issue of *Printing Impressions* magazine. I appreciated his kind words more than I was able to express. What an honor and humbling experience it was to spend some time with one of the greats in the printing industry!

We extend our deepest sympathy and eternal blessings to Mr. Dickeson's family. He will surely be missed!

—Philip P. Beyer

* Columnist, *Printing Impressions* magazine (1979 - 2006)

# TABLE OF CONTENTS

# INTRODUCTION

OVER THE PAST DOZEN YEARS I have had opportunity to see the power of industry, and the efforts of many who attempted to harness that power, clash like Titans in an arena. I have seen my own early attempts and frustrations reflected in the faces of others who have dared to own their own business, only to find them stressed to the point of despair. It doesn't have to be that way!

My reason for writing this book is to show even the most ordinary person how to organize, build and grow an extraordinary business through a systematic approach.

I spent ten years researching, considering, dissecting, building, measuring, tweaking, writing and implementing a system to bring order to my own business. I feel confident I can show you how you can eliminate bottlenecks, clean up messes, and make your business run like a super-clean, well-oiled machine, every single day from now until the end of time—whether you are there or not!

I waited to begin writing this book until I had *tested* these systems and *knew* they would actually work—to watch how they transform a company step-by-step. *We've done it.*

Using our commercial printing company as the prototype, we have been able to break down all facets of business systems that seem very complicated into something easy to understand.

Some systems are so simple I'm still amazed that more organizations have not implemented or even discovered them. I have proved to myself and others that any person who is willing to put their shoulder to the wheel—and not look back—can build a successful organization that will serve, educate, and be a model of excellence to the world.

OK, so at this point you may be thinking, "Oh, this book is for commercial printers, not for *my* type of business!" WHOA!!

*THIS BOOK IS FOR YOU if your answer is "Yes" to any of the following questions . . .*

- Troubled with CHAOS in your business?

- LOSING MONEY due to wasted time and resources?

- Stressed over MISTAKES recurring over and over?

- MISSED DEADLINES causing panic?

- Working LONG HOURS training and retraining personnel?

- OVERWORKED and no time for personal life?

- FRUSTRATED keeping your business clean and orderly?

- Constant INTERRUPTIONS with the same questions?

*THIS BOOK IS ALSO FOR . . .*

- Those who want to learn how to organize and turnkey any type of business or organization—service or manufacturing;

- Those who may not have a business education or training, but who have the drive and vision to launch their own business;

- Managers of small-to-large companies and organizations who want to improve their skills and see their company grow and prosper.

*AND FOR THOSE OF YOU who have many years of business education and experience,* I feel confident you will pick up a few priceless nuggets of fine gold—*they were mined under extreme pressure!*

## CHAPTER 1
# WHERE DO YOU START?

ACCORDING TO THE SMALL BUSINESS ADMINISTRATION (), over 50 percent of small businesses fail in the first year, and 95 percent fail within the first five years. A great many of these businesses fail in the fourth or fifth year, because they have usually grown to a size where the owner can no longer maintain proper control.

I started my business in 1988 and by my *fifth* year I was experiencing major problems. CHAOS!

I REALIZED I DIDN'T OWN A BUSINESS—IT OWNED ME!
I ONLY HAD A VERY DIFFICULT JOB.

Most business problems come to the surface after growing to a certain size, and then the floodgates of chaos are opened. You find your business is too large for you to keep all the information in your head. You still do most of the work, and your company is too small to hire the people you think you need to handle the chaos. As long as you are a one- or two-person operation, everything goes rather smoothly, but when you get to four or more employees—WATCH OUT!

I have included some true stories and anecdotes in this book because I believe they paint pictures that communicate complex ideas in a simple way. I worked literally thousands of hours for ten years, building a network of systems to systematize every aspect of our organization from top to bottom.

Not long ago I was talking with an older salesman from the largest manufacturer of printing presses in the world. He told me the thing he had come away with, after years of visiting hundreds of printing companies, is the wonder any job ever gets through the production and service processes correctly, due to nearly endless variables that must be considered, and their apparent lack of controls.

The greater wonder for me, after my own discussions with countless business leaders over the years, is why so many companies *remain* chaotic—and that, for most businesses, *chaos* is considered "normal."

Maybe you've found yourself caught up in that deception?

### A Day in the Life of Some American Businesses

Cranky opens his place of business at 8:00 A.M.—Salesman Bob arrives at 8:20; Worker Sue and Bookkeeper Mary get in around 8:45. Salesman Bob and Worker Sue answer the phones until CSR Jim wanders in at about 10 or so. Then Cranky answers the phone while Bookkeeper Mary sends Worker Sue to the bank, except on Tuesdays when Worker Sue takes "Scooter" to Doggie Daycare, then CSR Jim goes to the bank. But if CSR Jim is on call, then Bookkeeper Mary has to go herself—if she can borrow Cranky's car, since her teenage son wrecked hers.

Cranky takes care of doing payroll on Fridays, unless he is having lunch with a client—then Worker Sue will do it, because she always has, and Bookkeeper Mary was never trained on payroll.

CSR Jim takes calls and writes most of the job orders, unless he is called to the back of the shop to handle problems in production, and then Salesman Bob is asked to take the orders. But Salesman Bob doesn't like doing that, so sometimes he just lets the phone ring until Cranky has to answer and take the order himself. But when Cranky takes a job order he usually writes it up wrong, so CSR Jim gets mad at Salesman Bob for not doing the job, and Salesman Bob gets uppity and says *his* job is selling—and why should he have to answer phones and take in orders, anyway?

Cranky gets upset at CSR Jim and Salesman Bob for quarreling and says, "If Salesman Bob is too @#% busy, then we'll have

Worker Sue give us a hand, if her nails are dry and her stupid dog's OK!" As Cranky downs a blood pressure pill, they all wonder, "What is Cranky's problem—what is he so upset about?" I think you get the point. Chaos!

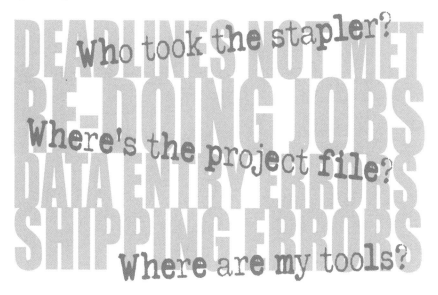

## So Where Do You Start, to Bring Order to Your Business?

You start by facing the truth—recognizing you have chaos, and admitting you need help bringing your business to order! Now you must make the decision to STOP the chaos or continue the pain!

Chaos is NOT "normal"—this book will help you
GET OVER IT!

Be aware, however—setting out on this adventure to totally systemize your operation, is not for the faint of heart; but I believe it will revolutionize your business and, quite possibly, your life!

# CHAPTER 2
## MY DAY OF DECISION

IN 1993 ONE OF OUR REGULAR CUSTOMERS stopped by my first print shop in Nashville, Tennessee, to have some copies made. As we were having a casual conversation, I noticed he was eyeing the shop with a less than approving look on his face. He finally said, "Philip, you need to clean this place up. It looks awful—and it does not make a very good impression!"

I was pretty embarrassed, to say the least, and felt a little defensive. After he left, I wondered, "Who does he think he is, coming into my shop and telling me how to run my business?" The more I thought about it, the madder I got.

As I was thinking about what had just happened, I turned and looked up on the wall and there was the large, ragged-edged sign I had posted a year or so earlier. The sign simply read, JOHN 3:16.

You may be familiar with this scripture verse that means a lot to me. Well, at that moment I had the distinct impression God was saying to me, "Philip, either bring order to this place, or take My name down. What the customer said to you is true!"

Yes, my company was in chaos, my nerves were on edge, and we were dropping balls left and right. We were making data entry errors and a lot of costly mistakes in production. Customers would call inquiring about a job in progress, and sometimes it would take us twenty minutes or more to locate it. Old jobs tickets that should have been filed, might take hours to locate, or had been completely lost.

The shop was cluttered and disorganized—I had so many papers on my desk they were falling off on the floor. I could hardly leave the shop without returning to major problems!

I had to admit I really didn't know how to organize even a small company with only four or five employees. That's a terrible place to be, knowing there's a big problem, but not knowing how to correct it or where to begin.

## An Answer Comes

A few weeks later one of my best friends, Van Thompson, who is also one of the founders of Griffin Technology in Nashville, came to the shop and noticed I was really stressed. I was complaining about the mess and the fact that I couldn't keep up with it all. Van wasted no time in asking me to take a ride with him. But I told him, "Van, I can't leave the shop, because every time I leave this place it costs me hundreds of dollars in mistakes." But, Van wouldn't take "no" for an answer and pressed me to "come on and take a ride. You need to get out of here for a while, and we'll be right back!"

I finally agreed to go with him, but with a first-class attitude.

I don't really remember where we went, but on the way back to the shop I noticed he was taking a detour to his house. I was getting pretty irritated and told him I didn't have time for that, but he said he'd only be a minute. When we pulled up to his house, he jumped out, ran inside, and soon came out with a book in his hand.

Throwing it on the front seat, he said, "Read this! It will help you with the shop."

Now he was getting on my last nerve! "I don't have time to read books," I barked. "I'm just too busy with the business and the rest of my life." But, I took the book home after work that day and set it aside. About two weeks later I decided to read before going to sleep, and there laid Van's book, *The E Myth* by Michael Gerber.

"Some title! What's the 'E' stand for?" I wondered, negatively. But I began to read, and as I got into the second chapter, I swear I bolted straight up in the bed. It was like a light had come on in my head. "I know what to do!" I said out loud, as if anyone was listening. "I know how we can fix this thing!"

It was just a simple story in the book about a man staying at a hotel, and the great service he had received—how the hotel had an actual *system* to make that great service happen.

Now, the book didn't tell me step-by-step how to fix or *turnkey* a company, but it gave me the spark needed to light the fire and the passion for a mission to fulfill the vision I believed God had placed in my heart.

All the years of being a self-employed *entrepreneur* came together with almost total understanding in just a moment of time. By the way, that's what that "E" in *E Myth* stands for—Entrepreneur!

I set out to find other books and information; also, the counsel of other business owners. I read everything I could put my hands on to help me prepare for the work ahead. I was determined to turn the vision into reality—and turn my company into a world-class operation. I couldn't wait to get started.

*In the day of my trouble I will call upon You,*
*and You will answer me.*
David, the Giant Killer

## TURNKEY

A franchise or business, complete with an operations manual,
purchased in a condition ready for immediate occupation;
whereas, the buyer only has to "turn the key"
for the operation to start

# CHAPTER 3
## BEGINNING THE MISSION

FACING THIS CHALLENGE HEAD-ON, I thought it was time to take a good, hard look at my own life.

Do I really seek truth, or do I avoid things I don't want to deal with? Do I procrastinate and sweep things under the carpet?

As an entrepreneur, do I jump from one project or business idea to the next, never totally completing anything? Do I really dot the 'i's and cross the 't's? Or do I approach things haphazardly, saying to myself, "It's not that important" or "It's so small, no one will ever notice?"

There's a story about Michelangelo, the painter, that one day his employer—who had commissioned him to paint the Sistine Chapel in Rome—noticed Michelangelo spending a significant amount of time in one dark corner of the building. He asked Michelangelo why he was being so meticulous when no one was likely to see it? Michelangelo simply replied, "*God* sees!"

Well, you may not think that's reason enough to do your best in *all* situations, but what I will reveal in this book will explain in detail the reasons you *should*.

As for me, I decided to face the *truth*, whatever the cost:

• I would insist on truth from myself and my employees, and not accept office politics in its place.

• No stone would be left unturned, seeking answers to our problems.

• I would continually improve the company through a systematic approach in every area of the business.

• I would continue my business education.

• I would keep up with new technologies to improve our business.

• I would refuse to be sidetracked with the latest trends or fads in the business world.

I made a promise to God and myself, I would not start another business venture that might take me away from my mission, until my company was totally turnkey and reflected His excellence.

I had no idea how long it would take. But, I guess, if you had told me then it would take over ten years, I might not have made the journey.

*I knew if I was going to commit to this, it all had to start with me—and I would have to change! And change, I did!*

I'm sure you've heard it said, "The truth will set you free!" Well, I've learned in business and in my life—that is absolutely true. Only when you know the truth about an issue or problem, can you *fix* it. If you don't believe in this concept, I suggest you put this book down, because from here on I only go deeper into the truth, and it will cost you. But, it's well worth it!

## Can it be done?

In the Graphic Arts industry the manufacturing process, from data entry to shipping, is extremely complicated. Each job is custom, and the variables seem almost infinite. I guess if you wanted to tackle something hard to organize and turnkey to the extent of the McDonald's Corporation, it would be a *commercial printing company*. In fact, when I first began to turnkey my company I was told by another printing company owner, "It can't be done; there are just too many variables!" To tell you the truth, in my second year of systemizing I started to believe I had taken on the impossible—but I pressed on.

*For which of you, intending to build a tower,*
*does not sit down first and count the cost,*
*whether he has enough to finish it?*
Luke the Physician

## Do I Need a Consultant?

Companies just starting out—those experiencing trouble, and owner/managers who find themselves overwhelmed and weary—often turn to motivational seminars and consultants to find answers. They hear the fine-sounding words of some who *seem* to have the cure for all their ills. Wisdom says we need to keep our ears open to *good* counsel, but here's where discernment is needed.

There are some exceptionally motivating speakers on the circuit, but there are also thousands of self-proclaimed "gurus"—I call them the "Rah-Rah boys"—who, if "busted," would prove to be less than the experts they make the big bucks to imitate. Beware of those who would move into your operation, make themselves what you think is "invaluable," and then bleed you dry.

If an "expert" does not have the heart to serve your best interests, and to see your company prosper without draining or taxing its resources, I would look elsewhere. In fact, I would recommend you run for your life!

As I contemplated writing this book, a friend of mine brought me the comic strip below. Funny, yes—but also sadly true!

Printed by permission:

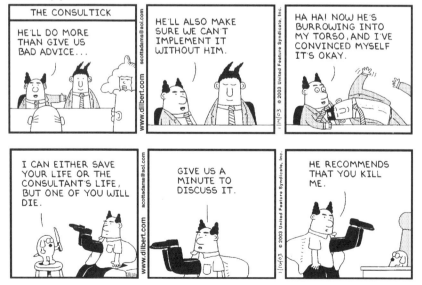

Dilbert by Scott Adams

Some consultants ("Consul*ticks*") give you systems only *they* can understand. They actually become part of the system they charge you to put in place. These particular ones expect you to continually rely on their "expertise" for your success. They want to become indispensable, so you won't remove them. Never turn over complete control to anyone! As owner, and head steward, you should retain responsibility for your own company.

The most important question you could ask these people is: *Have you actually, successfully built a company from the ground up and seen it thrive?*

I believe whole-heartedly, if you will continue reading this book, and implement the things that apply to your organization, you can build a world-class operation—without me or any Consul*tick*.

You've heard the old adage, "Give a hungry person a fish to eat and tomorrow they will need another fish, but give them a fishing pole and teach them to fish and they can feed themselves." I humbly offer you this book—my best fishing pole.

> *Confidence in an unfaithful man in time of trouble*
> *is like a broken tooth, and a foot out of joint.*
> King Solomon

# CHAPTER 4
## WRITING IT ALL DOWN

THE NIGHT I GOT THE REVELATION for how to fix what was wrong with my company, I knew I needed to write it all down so I could refer back to it:

• How do I want my company to look?

• How should I and my employees conduct ourselves?

• How can I guarantee great quality and service to my customers?

I made a list of character traits I thought would constitute a great employee and owner. I called it *Profile of the Ideal Owner or Employee*. See page 138. You may want to add to my list.

Later, we added a guideline for how we should conduct ourselves morally and ethically. See *Code of Ethics* on page 141.

*The Declaration of Independence*, *The Bill of Rights*, even *The Ten Commandments*, are written documents used as guides to build lives and a nation. A mission statement, along with many other supporting documents, can be used as a guide to build a great company. Each added document should build upon the mission statement; not drift away from it. See MISSION STATEMENT on page 140.

### A Written Document Keeps You on Course

The *Declaration of Independence* says all men are created equal. And yet, at the time it was written, there was slavery in our budding Republic. Does this mean the *Declaration of Independence* is of no value? Since some of the founding fathers were not totally living up to its standards, should we abandon it? God forbid!

Our *Constitution* and the *Declaration of Independence* were the vision for a great nation, written down by men—however, it takes time to fulfill a great vision. We are wise to keep going back to our founding documents as our guide.

Frederick Douglass, the black orator during the Civil War, used the great words and ideals of those documents to hold our government accountable, often admonishing them that they were not living up to those great written words and ideals.

Our nation's founding documents still guide our government today, and point out whether our laws are on course. Our courts and judges measure our laws against these documents. That's why we hear people ask if this or that law is "constitutional" or not. All other laws we might implement are gauged using the measuring stick we call *The United States Constitution*.

Your company's MISSION STATEMENT and CODE OF ETHICS should act as your founding documents—your "Constitution." All of your POLICIES should measure up against it. The word *constitution* actually means establishment or laying the foundation.

Everything in your company's written system—your OPERATIONS MANUAL—should strengthen your MISSION STATEMENT. A mission statement can become mere words on a piece of paper, or it can become a living document guiding you through the years of building a great company or organization.

Some have said a mission statement is just an old business trend. Many organizations have them, and you may have written one yourself. What generally happens to these statements is, they are framed and put on a wall, or they get lost in a desk drawer, but it seems few ever read them again. Some business owners and managers never really take their MISSION STATEMENT seriously. I guess they figure if they write it, and wait awhile, the mission will just happen—sort of like "evolution"?

I can tell you, after ten years of concentrated organization of our company: *order-from-chaos* doesn't just happen—*order left unattended returns to chaos*—ORDER takes creativity and hard work!

## System of Apology

One of my pet peeves is getting an apology from a company that provides bad product or service, when I know full well the company has no written systems in place to fix the problem, to make sure it doesn't happen again, and relies heavily on an over-used *system of apology*.

Yes, we also have to apologize from time to time. It troubles me when an error on our part affects one of our customers. The difference is, I know we will continue to improve our systems and fight the good fight to fix, if not totally eliminate, errors.

I know when we *do* have to apologize, it will not be the "norm," as with most non-systemized businesses.

When our company makes a mistake, we respond and resolve the issue quickly; then the error is documented, investigated, and fixed with a *written* system. You will find, when not dealing with internal chaos, you will have more time to help customers with *their* issues.

## Downloading

The sometimes complex system of processes that run your business needs to be documented—and these documents should be organized into an Operations Manual. This is the central location into which you should download all the information you have stored in your brain's computer over the years for how your business operates. (Read more on Operations Manuals in Chapter 9)

The problem with carrying your system of operations around in your head is, people in your business need regular access to that information in order to do their job, and will constantly need to interrupt you or others until they are able to access the information for themselves—via a written Procedure, Policy or Checklist, etc.

THAT'S WHY YOU ARE TIRED AND STRESSED—
WHY YOU CAN'T LEAVE THE BUILDING
WITHOUT THINGS FALLING APART!

It's very draining to be the mainframe computer that everyone in the organization plugs into, in order to retrieve information.

You shouldn't blame your employees if they can't remember your verbal instructions, or how to do a task in exactly the same way you would do it, if you never bothered to write it down in a procedure. It's no wonder they make mistakes and use you as a computer, telephone book, operations manual, map, etc.

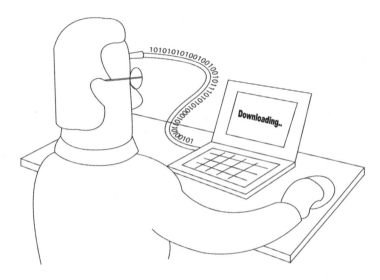

Imagine buying a complex machine without written instructions on how it operates. Think you would be calling the manufacturer, asking them countless questions? Your business is also a complex machine that needs written instructions to operate; without which, you can also expect operating errors and interruptions.

### You Can Write it Down

I was talking with my brother Teddy, an electrical engineer who owns his own business—Naztec. He commented that, "There are some things you just can't write down into a system."

I asked him to explain.

"Well," he said, "When I am ordering special parts that we assemble into products for our business, I look at every invoice to make sure we are getting good prices. When I order parts I know how to negotiate for a better price."

I suggested, as a designer of electronic circuits, he could easily write a system for purchasing—and recommended the following:

Make a list of the things you say while you're on the phone negotiating with these vendors for better prices. You could turn this into a checklist or procedure for your purchasing person or agent to use when buying. Maybe the lead statement—after the vendor has given your purchasing agent the price—is to tell them what price you paid last time, and you are hoping for a better price this time. Or, you could have your purchasing person call at least two or three vendors to get pricing. This would keep your main vendor accountable, while giving your purchasing person an edge in the negotiations.

I believe I know what my brother was trying to say. Simply stated, *you can't teach street smarts*—a shrewd awareness of how to negotiate and operate in a sometimes competitive or hostile situation; the ability to smell a trap a mile away and see through falsehood, or to discern subtle clues and know how to respond.

At some point, you MUST delegate tasks if you ever hope to have your company operate successfully and profitably without you being there, IF that's your goal. However, if you enjoy doing certain tasks or jobs, then by all means keep doing them.

Yes, in some circumstances the task you are trying to delegate may be a complex process that seems difficult to write into a procedure—but it's already in your head and you *can* write it down. You only have to write it down once, and then tweak it from time to time.

Do you realize you are freeing yourself from a particular job each time you finish writing a system and train someone to use it? You can literally work your way out of *all* jobs in your organization, if you are so inclined.

You may find you sleep better as you clear your mind of these processes. Have you ever had a hard time sleeping, because you keep going over and over something in your head? So you finally get up and make a list or write the thing down. Your brain has to work continually, expending a lot of your energy, to keep all the processes of your business fresh in your mind—not to mention all the new information you receive daily. Write it down!

*I can not stress strongly enough* the importance of downloading your business processes from your mind, into written documents— your OPERATIONS MANUAL.

As you build your manual, it will become more and more valuable—to you, to your employees, and the actual worth of your business. You will gain freedom from day-to-day operations you should not have been burdened with in the first place.

You are the vision person; you should be spending your time looking down the road to see what opportunities and hazards lie ahead. There will be many challenges on the world's business highway that is ever-changing, and with mind-bending speed. You will need to stay focused and not get bogged down by the daily functions of your business.

*If you can't describe what you are doing as a process,*
*you don't know what you're doing!*
W. Edwards Deming

# CHAPTER 5
# WORKING ON YOUR BUSINESS NOT IN IT

BY NOW I HOPE YOU CAN SEE, by working *on* your business and not just *in* your business, you will gain the freedom to do the things you have always wanted to do, but couldn't find the time or the energy.

A lot of owners are doing the work of two or more people. They spend eight to fourteen hours a day, or even more, working in one or more of the positions in their business.

*So HOW WILL YOU EVER FIND TIME TO WORK ON SYSTEMS TO REALLY ORGANIZE YOUR BUSINESS?*

You may not like the answer, but this is what I did:

I worked at least two to four hours *extra* each day and on weekends, designing systems to fix the *biggest* problems first.

After about two years, things really started to roll. About that time a friend and former business owner who was advising me at that time made a good observation. He noticed I was spending most of my day taking in orders or acting as an inside customer service representative. He said, "Philip, I really think if you would train someone to take *your* place—maybe your daughter-in-law—then you would have more time to work *on* your business."

I agreed, and started building systems for Customer Service and Order Entry; two positions I was doing myself. After building most of the systems for each of these positions—which consisted of a JOB DESCRIPTION, DAILY ROUTINE CHECKLIST, DATA/ORDER ENTRY

CHECKLIST, ESTIMATING CHECKLIST, POLICIES and PROCEDURES—I took the business owner's advice and hired my daughter-in-law, Jennifer. I trained her on these systems for three months, eight hours a day, until she was doing about 80 percent of my job. Wow! I had six extra hours a day to work on the business! Things really started to move, and as she improved I had even more time. Now I was mostly working in the position at the top of my ORGANIZATIONAL CHART (See page 142)—as Owner/President—and also as the Sales and Marketing Manager. I could not believe the transformation that began to take place.

Although it seemed natural to hire and train people to take other positions I had formerly occupied—such as Production Worker, Bookkeeper, etc.—I didn't think I would ever be free of actually doing the job of Customer Service, Purchasing and Production Manager. Those positions had given me the controls I thought I needed to make sure my business survived, because it had put me directly in contact with customers and vendors, and I also had control over production. I just couldn't see anyone else doing those jobs the way I would do them—until I understood the *power of systems*.

Freedom will come as you install good systems!

Once you hand those systems off to someone else—and you're not trying to be all things to all people—you will have the time to work on your vision of becoming a great organization.

Your new position will be to work ON your business, not IN it!

All those things most business owners long to do are not as far off as you think!

•More time for family

•Take a real vacation

•Serve in your community

•Spend time on personal projects

•Start another enterprise

•Write a book?

Working *on* your business will help you attain your goals and much more. No more spinning your wheels. You will truly *own* a business and not just have a job.

> *I spent my life stringing and unstringing my instrument,*
> *but the song I came to sing remains unsung.*
> Rabindranath Tagore - from his poem *Waiting*

## Entrepreneur, Manager, or Technician?

Michael Gerber's book, *The E Myth,* talks about three types of people in an organization—Entrepreneurs, Managers and Technicians. It's important to identify people's skills and interests, including your own, to make sure you have the right people in the right positions.

The ENTREPRENEUR envisions or starts an enterprise. They are self-starters. However, they sometimes lack organizational skills and, because of that, are not always adept at running a business. You see them going from one project to the next and sometimes never completing any of them. They can become bored quickly doing one thing, because they tend to be thinking about the *next* thing—a new invention, idea or project.

Entrepreneurs see opportunity around every corner, but often lack the discipline *not* to chase every rabbit they see. If you are an entrepreneur, organization may elude you, because you have too many irons in the fire or too many ideas going on at one time. You need managers and technicians to put feet to your ideas.

Think of your business as the invention of a new widget. Take your creative talent and focus it on building your business. Reinvent your business into the world's best-run "widget." After you turnkey your business, you may want to sell it and then move on to the next widget.

The MANAGER tends to have good leadership and organizational skills that help to build the business. Their work is to manage and improve the system, and sometimes to *create* systems.

A manager should be trained NOT to manage *people*, but to manage the *systems* that will, in turn, manage the people.

The TECHNICIAN has the skills to do the hands-on work of the organization—or you could say they shape the stones and move them into place. The technician's work is to operate the system and play a vital role in its improvement.

*Please note:* A system doesn't know an Entrepreneur, from a Manager, from a Technician, from a cow in the road.

The system will only work as long as everyone uses it correctly, and a good system should signal when you are NOT.

In the best system—all parts work together as *one*!


*What a strange thing a body would be*
*if it had only one part!*
*The eye can never say to the hand, "I don't need you."*
*The head can't say to the feet, "I don't need you."*
Paul the Tent Maker

## CHAPTER 6
# WHAT ARE SYSTEMS?

### A Vision of Circles

I WAS ABOUT TWENTY-EIGHT YEARS OLD and sitting on my front porch in Louisiana one night, when I had what I thought was a very real vision. Looking up at the stars, I envisioned what seemed to be perfect circles of all sizes. All of the circles intersected and seemed to interact with one another. It struck me that each circle affected every other circle—or system—in the universe. It also occurred to me that everything in the universe was represented by these circles, and the circles represented systems. That was it! That was my vision. What to *do* with all that, remained a mystery to me until years later when I began systemizing my company, and then it began to make sense.

Taking it further . . . our planet, the solar system, all the stars and galaxies are actually *systems* of circles—each planet affecting the other planets, just as one galaxy affects another galaxy, and so on into infinity. It's all connected.

Well, back to earth!

Just as a circle with gaps in it is not a *complete* circle—a system with a gap in it is also incomplete; it will not work properly. The more you refine and close the gaps in a system, the more continually it will work, with less and less effort.

The most frequently asked question I get from business owners and managers regarding systems is, "Once you build your systems, how do you get people to consistently use them?"

They put a system in place, it works for awhile, then it stops working and people go back to their old habits. I tell them, the reason it stops working is because they haven't completed the circle—there are GAPS in the system. The gap is, they have no *follow-up system* to insure people are staying the course.

## So, What IS a System?

THE SYSTEM, as defined in this book, is a network of interacting written PROCEDURES, POLICIES, CHECKLISTS, etc., to create an OPERATIONS MANUAL for a business—the processes that run your company.

This OPERATIONS MANUAL is made accessible to every member of your organization, to give clear understanding to all—empowering them to do their job without constant supervision.

## Webster's Dictionary Defines Systems:

1.  A group or arrangement of parts, facts, phenomena, etc., that relates to or interacts with each other in such a way as to form a whole;
2.  An orderly method, plan or procedure.

    I call them LIFESAVERS!

Another way to think of a system is like a circuit board an engineer designs and then tests until it works perfectly. It should not have any breaks in the circuit, unless it is a *planned* break.

The engineer then puts this new circuit board—along with additional parts with which the circuit board interacts—into a nice clean package, and the new electronic widget works every time you turn it on. No need to go back to the schematic, unless it needs repair. If you forget how a particular feature operates, you simply refer to the OPERATIONS MANUAL.

Imagine, turning on your new electronic widget and it stopped working every few minutes—and you had to bang on it or take a wire and jump one of its circuits to get it working again. Well, that's how companies operate without good business systems. You need to take the time to ensure your processes work flawlessly, by testing how each system affects all other systems.

The right system completes the circuit 100 percent, like a *circle* with no gaps. *Less* than 100 percent and it will not work properly.

### *COMPLETE*

*Having all needed or normal parts, elements or details—*
*lacking nothing. Entire, thoroughly wrought, finished. Perfect!*

A close friend of mine said it like this, "A business without good systems is like a body without a central nervous system—lots of loose nerve ends reaching for something that doesn't exist." I call the operation of that kind of company the "Anti-System Solution."

**The mindset of the "Anti-System Solution" is . . .**

- Systems are for very large organizations only—or not necessary at all.
- You need good people—not good systems.
- The answer to the problem is: more customers bringing in more business.

You might imagine one of these "Anti-System Solution" companies sending out a series of MEMOS FROM MANAGEMENT that read like the following:

**MEMO**: Due to lost revenue, a powerful marketing campaign will be launched to bring in more business.

**MEMO:** Due to more chaos from all this new business, more meetings will be scheduled to deal with customer and employee frustrations over production and service problems.

**MEMO:** Due to production and service problems, new managers are being hired to handle the chaos.

**MEMO:** Due to the lack of profits from soaring marketing and management costs, we need to reduce budgets in the following areas: employee salaries, service maintenance and new equipment acquisitions.

**MEMO**: Due to a lack of skilled labor from budget cuts, managers will be expected to fill in the gaps.

**MEMO:** Due to budget cuts for maintenance and new equipment, we are experiencing more equipment breakdowns causing further employee frustration . . . bringing about employee turnover . . . which is creating missed deadlines . . . which is also resulting in lost customers.

**MEMO**: Due to lost customers and red ink, a powerful marketing campaign will be launched to bring in more business. Also a NEW AND IMPROVED consultant has been hired to work onsite to determine the problem.  P.S. Our consultant has asked us not to call what we are experiencing *"problems"—but, "opportunities."*

*Do you know a business that is experiencing*
*those kinds of "opportunities?"*

Before you finish reading this book, you will have seen many examples of systems that will help you get started in eliminating chaos in your own business. Stay with me!

It's your decision: THE SYSTEM—or THE ANTI-SYSTEM?

# CHAPTER 7
# IF NOT SYSTEMS, WHAT?

## Managers, Managers, Managers

EVER WONDER WHY many companies are top-heavy with managers and assistant managers? In many cases, it's due to a lack of proper systems—so they hire managers to manage the chaos.

As I described in the previous chapter, a gap or hole in a company's system is where a bottleneck can happen. Instead of building a system without gaps, companies hire managers to push the wheel of production and service to get it rolling again when it gets bogged down or stops in the gaps. Then another manager will push it again when it stops at the next gap, and so on. They will even hire an assistant manager to help the manager when the gap is too big for one person to keep it rolling. So, instead of putting a good system in place, they insert more and more managers into the gaps.

The actual job of any manager should be to *know* and *endorse* a company's system; *to improve* and to *teach* the system—and to ensure all employees are *adhering* to the system, so operations will continue to run smoothly.

It should never be the job of a manager, to run to and fro managing chaos, putting out fires—being a *gap-plugger*—and instructing or reminding people again and again about what, when, where, how, and how much.

Again, managers are most effective when they manage the company's system; which, in turn, will manage the people; thereby, managing the chaos.

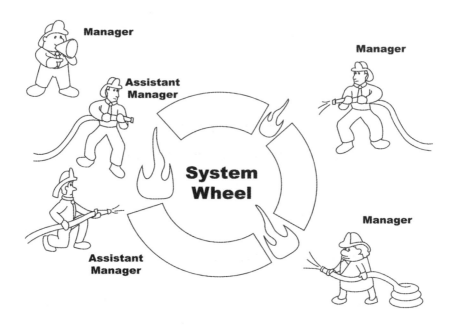

## The Wrong Type of Manager

One manager I hired had come from a company that was somewhat larger than our company. He had managed a department with fifty or more employees, and had experienced burn-out at his former company, because in order to keep up he had consistently worked sixty to seventy hours a week. He wanted to move to the south, so he answered an ad we had placed for a Pre-Press Manager. Let's call him "Sam."

We thought Sam was the answer to helping us meet the goals we had set for the Pre-Press Department. Even before his arrival we had the Pre-Press Department very clean and systemized. We trained him on our system and we believed, certainly with his background, his running our well-systemized Pre-Press would be a cinch. But, after he was with us for two or three weeks the department started to deteriorate. Our Customer Service personnel were becoming concerned, and THE SYSTEM said we had a problem in Pre-Press.

I called Sam into a meeting and he seemed to be very cooperative. "Sam, these are the concerns I have . . ." He wrote them down and said he would correct them immediately, but nothing changed. In fact, it was getting worse by the day, so I called him to my office again. This time he started complaining about "too many hours." I went over our concerns again and he said he would take care of them. A week or so later he was called out of town on an emergency and I told our Production Manager I wanted to run the Pre-Press until he returned. It would give me the opportunity to see how far the systems had actually broken down, and to find out why Sam was struggling.

I found Sam's desk and other Pre-Press storage cabinets in complete chaos. Notes he had taken in our meetings, and other important papers, were just buried in the bottom of drawers. I realized he was the type of manager who just hid things, instead of dealing with issues. I also found he had lost a lot of our Pre-Press templates and had disregarded other systems we used as major time savers. None of them were being utilized. He was *off* the system and that was the reason for the problems we were having.

When he returned to the office I met with him again. I said, "Sam, I understand why you are working the long hours you have been complaining about. *You have departed from our system* and now you're way off course." I told him that while he was gone, and I was working in his place, I had started a job and found the Pre-Press templates missing, so I had to start the job from scratch. It had taken me three extra hours to complete it and I believed he had been doing it from scratch every time.

"Do you know how many hours you lose a week, not using the template system?" I asked. He informed me he had lost the templates, so I asked him why he had not rebuilt them. He had no answer, just a blank stare. That seemed to account for many of the extra hours Sam said he needed to work. I estimated that Sam was losing ten to fifteen hours a week, by not using the system correctly.

When we fail to file things, and bury them in a drawer or cabinet, it causes turmoil later and more time can be lost!

"Sam, I am totally confused!" I said. "How did you run the entire production of a company four times the size of ours?"

He said, "Oh, I had several assistant managers and they helped me with much of the work."

Hmm! Managers, Managers, Managers!

I said, "Sam, don't you realize, if you would stick to the system you wouldn't have to work sixty or seventy hours a week?" I was convinced he would not have needed all those assistant managers at his old company if he'd had an excellent system, and adhered to it.

Yes, I had to give him his leave, but I still considered it constructive for me to have gone through that with Sam. Our follow-up systems had saved our company valuable time and money by revealing this manager's actual lack of management skills before it became detrimental. Sometimes people look you in the eye, as Sam did, and say, "Yes, I'll take care of that," but their actions say "No!" They are betting no one will follow up on them.

*I walked by the field of a lazy person,*
*the vineyard of one lacking sense.*
*I saw that it was overgrown with thorns.*
*It was covered with weeds,*
*and its walls were broken down.*
*Then, as I looked and thought about it,*
*I learned this lesson: A little extra sleep,*
*a little more slumber, a little folding of the hands to rest*
*and poverty will pounce on you like a bandit.*
Solomon the Wise

## Meetings, Meetings, Meetings

You ask, "Why do some companies have so many meetings?" Again, most of the time it's because they don't have good systems. Every organization has problems, and meetings are the conventional way businesses deal with them. Generally, meetings are called to get everybody on the same page, or to remind people of things they thought would have been handled after the last meeting.

*A meeting may go like this . . .*

Sally forgot something a customer had requested and blames Joe. Joe blames Bob and Bob blames Sue, but they seem to get it all worked out in a lengthy meeting, which just cost the company a lot of money. The cost—number of people in the meeting, multiplied by their salaries, for the time spent in the meeting. And the next week it starts all over again. Someone calls another meeting because there are more problems to deal with, and some of the old problems are back again.

It can cost companies hundreds to thousands of dollars for a single meeting. Next time you are in a meeting, run some numbers to see how much that meeting costs.

Meeting time should be spent brain-storming or doing other visionary work, not putting out fires; meeting again and again with people just to instruct them to "remember" to do this or that.

If the issues that you hoped to resolve in meetings were placed in a written system—i.e. Daily Routine Checklists, Procedures, Policies, or other control checklists—most meetings would not be needed at all. Committing work details to memory alone is gambling with the results.

Again, scheduled meetings should be used to improve systems, boost morale, and for other creative work. This type of meeting is really productive, because they don't just rehash recurring problems—problems are fixed permanently and ideas are born.

Think how much money you would save with fewer meetings!

# CHAPTER 8
# WHY BE COMMITTED TO A SYSTEM?

WITH A GOOD SYSTEM, people in your organization have a clear understanding of the work they are to perform and what is expected of them. Without a system, there are many unanswered questions, and quality and service cannot be guaranteed.

Most companies don't have a written system of operation that provides employees the proper tools to accomplish their job. In these types of companies, when the management changes, the entire system may change.

You may have been in a situation where, if there's a qualified manager, operations run more smoothly. But if an unqualified manager comes along later, operations start falling apart. With a written system, operations remain stable—expectations and standards remain the same, no matter *who* the manager is. THE SYSTEM should set the agenda.

## Whose System is it?

We had a manager (I'll call her Helen) who was in charge of all the production departments. She was loved by the customers and had the respect of the employees. Everyone said she "ruled the roost." But Helen was beginning to have some personal issues and came to me with her resignation. I didn't want her to leave—however, I understood her situation. Other managers and employees in our company were coming to me with their concerns, asking, "What are we going to do without Helen?" I told them Helen, although a fine and capable person, was not the main reason things ran so well in production. It was the *systems* we had been building for nine years, at that time, that were the reason production ran so well. Helen's title was Production Manager, but—according to our systems—that meant she managed the PRODUCTION MANAGEMENT SYSTEM. Do you understand what I just said? Helen managed THE COMPANY PRODUCTION MANAGEMENT SYSTEM. It wasn't the HELEN PRODUCTION MANAGEMENT SYSTEM.

We had built a system for our company that was very detailed and complete. We completed the circuit, or circle, by removing the gaps in the production management wheel to keep it rolling along smoothly. The person who replaced Helen was trained quickly on the PRODUCTION MANAGEMENT SYSTEM. In fact, it ran better and with less effort—because we keep improving the system. This production management change was more confirmation for our employees, as to the importance of great systems.

Do you think McDonald's Corporation, the hamburger giant, changes their whole way of managing—or changes their system—when they change managers, personnel or even franchise owners? NO WAY! The new managers and personnel learn the McDonald's system. They follow the system and in turn are checked by the managers of the system to make sure they are adhering to that system. However, McDonald's franchise owners and all levels of personnel are encouraged to help improve the system—but first they learn the present system.

### Coffee Break at McDonald's

My son Paul and I decided to grab a cup of coffee at a McDonald's store right up the street from our business. While standing in line, I noticed empty coffee creamers piling up by the self-serve coffee pots, making a mess. I said, "Hey, Paul, look—a breakdown in the McDonald's system! They should put a container there with a small sign or label that says, PLACE YOUR EMPTY COFFEE CREAMERS HERE."

A few days later we had to laugh when we were back getting a cup of coffee. There it was—without us saying a word, someone had added a container and a sign: PLACE YOUR EMPTY COFFEE CREAMERS

HERE. It was a great little demonstration of how the system of continual improvement works. But let's break it down a little further.

## THE COMPANY—as a Reason to Be Committed to a System

What is the main reason a business is in business? It's to make a profit, right? In some corners of today's society it seems *profit* has become a dirty word. However, making a profit has to be the main goal in order for the company to exist—but, not the only goal.

With a successful company that makes profits, you can afford to give back to your community in countless ways. If it weren't for many great American companies, we wouldn't have some of the schools, libraries, hospitals, research centers and many other blessings those profits have provided—not to mention the jobs they create. These companies have also been used in times of war to maintain our freedoms. Therefore, to help assure prosperity—which I believe is profit with peace and joy attached—you need a great system.

## THE CUSTOMER—as a Reason to Be Committed to a System

If you promise great quality and service to customers, then you need a system to back it up. Therefore, you're able to prove your promise and it's not just a slogan on your business card. A good system is the only proven way to obtain consistent results—and it helps the sales and marketing department bring in more customers.

Later in the book you will read about how a Nintendo™ quality inspector described our operation as one of the cleanest and most organized printing companies he had ever seen. Our sales department had prospected and delivered the Nintendo™ customer to our door, but it was THE SYSTEM that helped close the deal.

A company delivering good quality and service at a fair price should be able to grow. And with the right marketing, you will grow! THE SYSTEM will help you guarantee that quality and service.

## THE EMPLOYEE—as a Reason to Be Committed to a System

A system lets management know which employees are performing well and which are not.

Performance should not be based on a *feeling* you get about how someone is performing—it should be based on *facts* that come from having a system that measures performance.

Have you ever been in a situation where you were working very hard and the person next to you was a slacker? Somehow, the supervisor never seemed to notice this person's laziness, because when the supervisor would come around, this person would kick up a lot of dust and pretend they were working very hard. The right system will expose such a person.

A diligent employee should have a sense of relief that good performance is also being noticed, because it is being documented.

A good system is one that encourages employees to become involved in improving their work area and processes.

If you measure an employee's ability on a scale of one to ten—a "five"with a great system could be as effective as an "eight" or a "nine." Just imagine what the same system could do for an employee who was already an eight or nine! As the system improves and transforms the organization, the people the organization attracts will improve.

### Attracting the Cream of the Crop

I had been looking for a top department manager for our company to take us further up the road on our mission. I came down to several choices—however, I had one person in mind. He was the kind of applicant you know is looking for a great company and not just a job. Before asking him to make a final commitment, I decided to give him a detailed orientation, which included a two-hour video, demonstrating our systems and a complete overview of our company (See Chapter 10, Orientation System).

After the orientation and a tour of our facility, he accepted the job saying, "This is the kind of company I've been looking for!" Again, the system sold the company—this time to an employee—and I didn't have to make any promises, exaggerate our good points or downplay our weak points.

*We are who we say we are!*

## The Anti-Employee Mind-set

I remember a business associate asking me to come over to his shop, to help him set up a printing press. After arriving and starting to work on his machine, to my frustration I realized the owner didn't have the proper tools to do the job. I asked him, "How do you expect me to set up your machine with just a few broken tools?"

He said the reason he didn't have any tools was, his employees had lost or taken them, and he wasn't going to buy more. Later, I went to the sink to wash my hands and found only a bar of soap to remove the ink, and then found nothing with which to dry my hands. I had to use the dirty shop towels I had just been using to clean the press. At our company, providing a special (albeit costly) ink-removing hand cleaner *and* paper towels is a given.

This owner had complained to me many times that he couldn't find good employees. Now I could see why! The guy was losing a dollar trying to save a dime. If you have this mind-set, you will likely never achieve a great organization or work environment. You're saying to your employees, "You are not important!"

## Good Employees Are Worth It

For our employees, we have a break room fixed up like a 1950s diner with counters, stools, tables and booths. It also has great memorabilia from the '50s era. When I built this for the employees I had several people tell me it was "overkill"—that the employees would not take care of it; and, in fact, they would abuse it. I didn't believe that would happen, and it didn't. The employees really enjoy it because, as they say, they feel like they have "left the building" when they go there for lunch or a break. It's fun to select a few 1950s tunes on the old Seeberg wall boxes and sit in a booth with your sandwich and a glass of cold Coca Cola™. All the amenities are supplied—coffee, assorted candy, etc. It's all free.

Good employees are worth it!

*The laborer is worthy of his reward.*
Apostle Paul

# CHAPTER 9
# HOW TO BUILD SYSTEMS
# AND
# YOUR OPERATIONS MANUAL

## To Build or Not To Build

First, you need to identify which events are causing the most frustration, such as errors, missed deadlines, and other problematic events that keep recurring. Next, determine whether these events are *predictable* and *preventable*—if yes, you build a new system or improve a current system to prevent them from happening. There is, of course, no system you could build—i.e. checklist, procedure etc.- to stop an *unpredictable* and *unpreventable* event, such as an Act of God. However, you can implement a disaster recovery program to minimize the damage—i.e. emergency backup batteries to keep telephones, servers and emergency lighting, etc. operating for a while.

## Start With the Biggest Hole

Think of a ship that's been in battle and has holes everywhere and water pouring in. Does this sound like any business you know? Which hole would you plug first?

In our case, the biggest holes needing plugged were mistakes in our pressroom. So I built a QUALITY CONTROL CHECKLIST for the press operators and immediately it stopped many of the large leaks.

I then moved upstream to plug the next biggest leak, and developed a checklist for entering jobs into production. I continued up and down the process stream until we had stopped all major leaks.

To keep the improvement process moving forward, I needed a

system to find small and almost undetectable leaks. I developed a system that would catch these problems—which I call System Busters—that most companies would never find, much less fix. More on SYSTEM BUSTERS in Chapter 11.

## The Spinning Plates

You may have seen the circus performer who spins ceramic plates on a row of long poles. He puts a plate on a pole, gives it a spin, then moves on to the next pole and spins another plate, and so on. Sometimes, as he is spinning a new plate, one of the first plates falls to the ground. So he runs back and puts on a new plate and gives it a spin. There's a point in the act where the performer is running up and down the row trying to keep all the plates spinning. He seems anxious and frantic for a time, but when he gets them all spinning he is all smiles, because now all he has to do is *walk* up and down the row giving each plate a gentle tap with his finger to keep them all spinning merrily without falling off the poles.

This is how it will seem when you are setting up systems for your organization. Just when you think you have a system working, it will crash—but don't give up. Just pick it up, find out why it stopped operating, fix it, and move on. It's not like you have to build the system from the ground up each time. Once all your systems are up and running—you only have to tweak them now and then.

## THE BUILDING BLOCKS OF A SYSTEM

Things to consider as you build your system:

## Context and Understanding

The words you use must plainly describe the actions and activity to be performed so any member of your organization can easily understand. The following story should illustrate what I mean.

It was told to me that during the Civil War, a famous Southern general had a certain private stationed right outside his tent. The private was a soldier of below-average intelligence. To be blunt, he was not the brightest button on a uniform. Well, when the general would write out specific orders to be sent to the front lines, he would send for this private to read the orders. He would then ask the private to tell him what they meant, in the private's own words. If the private had any trouble understanding what the general had written, the general would take the orders back and rewrite them. He would repeat this process until the private could easily explain to him what his orders stated. The general knew if *this* private could understand his orders, surely when his officers on the front lines received the orders, they would understand them, too.

It is *imperative* that a manager understands every word and sentence in every system in their department.

An owner or general manager should have an overall understanding of the entire system.

> *Easy reading is hard writing.*
> Nathaniel Hawthorne

Another illustration of context and understanding is the story about an unexplainabe box. I was having our online BILL OF LADING system programmed for our SYSTEM100™ software. As I was reading all the information, and looking at the different boxes to be filled in on the bills of lading from several freight lines we used, I realized I didn't know the use of a particular box. The box had a header, but its purpose was unknown to me. I asked our shipping manager to explain the purpose of the box on the form and she couldn't tell me. I decided to call one of the freight lines and ask them what the purpose of the box was. They couldn't tell me either—and it was *their* form.

I called other freight lines and got the same answer. No one could tell me what the box was used for or why it was there. One company put me in touch with their legal department, as I wanted to make sure the bill of lading form we were drafting was acceptable, and I wanted to know what that dumb box was. The legal department could not explain why it was there and, in fact, joked about it.

The moral of this story? Know each word and sentence—or dumb box—in your system.

## Participation

Before a system is implemented you should let everyone this system/document will affect share their ideas, so they know how it will impact their job. These same people should also be involved in the testing, revising and updating of the system.

## Standardization

All references and terms should be used the same way, every time. For example, don't call something in one system or form a *cell phone,* and in the next line call it a *mobile phone.* When you have hundreds of terms it can get very confusing. Also, it would be helpful to standardize your fonts; only using one or two. Be consistent.

## Completeness

There must be no gaps in information, logic, or design, as illustrated by another story I call *"Roadie Proof"*—it comes from my old rock 'n' roll performing days, with long hair and shiny clothes.

We had a PA sound system that was very elaborate—it had many powerful amplifiers that hooked up to lots of speakers, microphones, etc. If the wrong cable was plugged into the wrong speaker it would blow out the speaker. We had a couple of "roadies" for awhile who helped set up our equipment. We were barely scratching out a living, and the roadies were probably living with their parents and had not yet learned the art of decision-making.

One night, one of these roadies plugged in a cable from a 1000-watt amplifier to a speaker that was rated to handle about 200 watts. Yes, it blew up! Being the resourceful and handsome young band-leader that I was, I decided to fix this problem myself. Truth is, there was no money for these kinds of mistakes. Truth is, I wasn't quite as handsome as I thought I was, either!

Anyway, I went to an electronics store and bought four different types of plugs. We wired one cable with one type of plug, and the next cable with another type, and so on. It was now impossible to wire a cable to the wrong speaker. It just wouldn't fit. You know, like putting a square peg in a round hole. So, I coined the term "Roadie Proof," that stuck. Now when I explain how a system needs to be set up so it's almost impossible to mess up, my employees know exactly what I mean when I say we need to "Roadie Proof" this or that system.

The following is an example of a system with no gaps—a complete system for Ordering Materials:

Each person in each department, in fact all employees, should have a DAILY ROUTINE CHECKLIST—a list of every task an employee does each day. More on DAILY ROUTINE CHECKLISTS, Chapter 10.

We will place on the checklist an entry with a check box beside it to remind (e.g.) a <u>production worker</u> to order  materials:

☐ Materials needed have been checked off on *Material Order Form* PD-343
  and completed form place in designated location

Every department has a MATERIAL ORDER FORM that has listed on it every item used on a regular basis in that department or work area. On this MATERIAL ORDER FORM there will be a description of the product, product number, quantity to order, etc. The only thing you—any staff member—is required to do is to review the list of items on this form, put a check in the box beside the item you want to order, and place the form in a designated location. Easy!

Next, the <u>purchasing person</u> will pick up the MATERIAL ORDER FORM and orders all materials that day—because the purchasing person has an entry on their DAILY ROUTINE CHECKLIST to do so.

☐ *Material Order Forms* PD-343 have been picked up from each department's
  designated location. All selected items have been purchased.

The purchasing person won't have to look for the description, the product number or how much to order, because all the information they need is already on the MATERIAL ORDER FORM. Easy!

*Note: Have you ever wasted thirty minutes or more looking for an old product box to get the description or product number of an item you need to reorder? That is lost time and money!*

Next, your materials will be delivered to your department, placed in a designated location, because it's on the <u>Shipping &</u>

Receiving person's DAILY ROUTINE CHECKLIST to deliver these items
to each department as they receive them.

> ☐ All Materials received have been distributed and placed in each
>    departments' designated location for materials received.

Now, do you see how one system works with and can affect
another system? A system should be designed to be easy to use and
work consistently—but, most importantly, it must be *complete*, like
a complete circuit. The easier it is to use, the more consistently
people will use it.  Let's review:

Step 1—Production Worker has an entry on their DAILY ROUTINE
CHECKLIST to order their needed materials.

Step 2—Purchasing person has an entry on their DAILY ROUTINE
CHECKLIST to pick up checked MATERIAL ORDER FORMS from each
department's designated location. Another entry on their CHECKLIST
is to order materials at a certain time of the day.

Step 3—Shipping & Receiving person has an entry on their DAILY
ROUTINE CHECKLIST to deliver ordered materials to the various designated locations when received.

## Compliance

There needs to be a way to follow up on systems to insure that a
system is being used—and used consistently. We have several
follow-up systems (See Chapter 11).

## Referencing

You need to connect or reference the system/document to other
frequently-used documents that will guarantee it will not be lost and
forgotten. Out of sight, out of mind is true!

As we built our Operations Manual, sometimes, when writing a
Policy or Procedure, it became apparent that we had already written
that same Policy or Procedure. We had simply forgotten it had been
done, and it was already in our Operations Manual. This happened
several times and it became very frustrating.

Even though we are constantly updating our OPERATIONS MANUAL, there are those systems/documents which are used for specific situations and they are only needed once or twice a year.

I was going over some of the documents with a new manager and he asked if we had a particular document. I told him we didn't, but we could easily implement one. I had him draw up a rough draft of what he wanted, and had someone create the document. As we started talking with other employees in the company to see how this new document would affect other systems, somebody said, "Hey, we already have that document."

Well, I went back to my office even more frustrated, but decided right then and there we would reference every system/document we had to other relative system/documents being used. When you reference those that are rarely used, to those that are used daily, they are not lost and forgotten. Since every system/document has a document number and a title, it was easy to start implementing.

I just looked at it as continual improvement for our OPERATIONS MANUAL.

## Final Approval

Remember, if others are assigned the task of building a system, YOU—the head of the organization—should give the final approval. And YOU need to know exactly how the new system is designed to work. *It starts at the top!*

## Organizing Your Operations Manual

We suggest using D-Ring binders to store hard copies of each department's OPERATIONS MANUAL. Each document in a binder should be placed in a clear sheet protector for easy removal when copying and updating. If your company is very small, or you are just starting a business or organization, you could start with one large D-ring binder and have tabs for each department until it becomes too full, then you can break out each department with its own binder.

Again, I would suggest using no more than one or two fonts on your documents. We use Arial for content, and Zapf Dingbats BT for checkboxes and other symbols. Helvetica is also a good font to use.

Remember, standardization is the name of the game in your OPERATIONS MANUAL.

For *document management*, I recommend all of your forms and documents be built in Microsoft Word. However, for very complicated forms you may consider other design programs.

Your MASTER LIST OF DOCUMENTS for your OPERATIONS MANUAL can be built in a Microsoft Excel spreadsheet, and each department's list of documents should have its own tab in the spreadsheet.

All companies have common departments, even if you are a very small operation—Sales, Human Resources, Accounting, etc.

In each department's D-ring binder, the first plastic sheet protector should contain a printed list (from your Excel spreadsheet) of the forms or documents for that department. Example below:

| Human Resources HR-1000 | | Date Updated 8/12/2010 | | |
|---|---|---|---|---|
| **Document Title** | **Document Number** | **Paper Stock** | **Text Color** | **Finishing** |
| Employment Application | S100-HR-1000 | 20# White Bond | Black | None Required |
| HR Manager-Job Description | S100-HR-1001 | 20# White Bond | Black | None Required |

This compiling and organizing of documents and forms into an OPERATIONS MANUAL is called forms or document management.

Now give each document a specific number, along with a revision date. Example: **YCI-HR-1001 Rev 09/10**:

**YCI** = Your Company Inc.

**HR** = Human Resources Dept

**1001** = Number you assign to that document

**Rev** = Revision date **09/10**

If you have a better way of doing it, great! I would suggest you put zeros in front of your single- or double-digit numbers so that, in the event you sort them in Excel or another program, they will line up. They will also sort correctly when you name your files and file folders on your computer. You should create a folder for each department. Example: 009, 010 and *not* 9, 10, etc. Do a test by sorting your form numbers in Microsoft Excel and you will get the idea.

## Recap of the Building Blocks of a System

**A.** Determine if a system needs to be built.

    1. PREDICTABLE EVENT

        • We update or build a new system, if not already addressed in the current system.

    2. UNPREDICTABLE EVENT

        • No reason to build system. Outside disruptions, client or vendor errors, Acts of God, etc.

**B.** Fix the "biggest hole" first. Prioritize those areas of frustration that need to be systemized.

**C.** Make changes/updates to system only if it:

    1. Stops errors and chaos not previously encountered

    2. Streamlines the process

    3. Standardizes the process

    4. Stops the problem of forgetting process steps or tasks

    5. Saves time and/or cost

**D.** As you begin to develop or improve a system:

    1. Consider all personnel involved or affected by that process.

    2. Write down the process step-by-step as you think it would make the most sense.

    3. Think about the flow of the process and how each step effects the next step. "Roadie Proof" the process.

    4. Each person affected by the system/document is given a copy to review each step in the process, looking for gaps or holes. They will then give their input, as to whether it works smoothly or needs to be revised. It's important they clearly understand each step as in the story of *The General and the Private.*

    5. Once the needed changes have been made in the system, everyone will review it again. Repeat Steps 3 and 4 until every one is satisfied with the results.

6. Be sure the system/document has a follow-up system.

7. Assign a document number and a revision date.

8. Reference the system/document to other frequently-used documents to guarantee it will not be lost and forgotten.

9. The Systems Manager/Head of Organization should give final approval.

*Through wisdom a house is built and
by understanding it is established.*
Old Proverb

# CHAPTER 10
# TYPES OF SYSTEMS THAT EMPOWER PEOPLE

## JOB DESCRIPTIONS

AN ORGANIZATION OR BUSINESS should have a detailed job description—a list of specific tasks and responsibilities—for each and every position/person in the organization. Some job descriptions may include several positions. In smaller companies, one person may wear many hats.

When we started building our OPERATIONS MANUAL we had only four or five job descriptions for our entire company. Some positions were combined. Example: <u>Press Operator and Bindery Operator</u>; another was <u>Delivery Driver and Shipping/Receiving</u>, etc. As you grow you may have one position for each person.

## DAILY ROUTINE CHECKLIST

This document is like the job description, developed into a detailed checklist of duties in the order a person performs them, from the time they arrive at work until they leave. It is to be prominently located for easy use, either on an employee's desk or a clipboard at their workstation. With this document you—the owner or manager—also have for your reference a list of everything each employee does. You don't have to ask someone what a particular employee does, or try to remember it yourself, as it is all written down. This can be very helpful when one of your employees tells you they have too much to do. If you agree with them, since your business may be growing, it's easy enough to review their DAILY

ROUTINE CHECKLIST and make a decision to transfer a certain task or duty to someone else. Just add, delete or exchange a task from one DAILY ROUTINE CHECKLIST to another. The task may be a better fit for someone else, or for one who doesn't have as much on their plate.

You see, the DAILY ROUTINE CHECKLISTS are your eyes to see every task and duty performed in your organization—from taking the mail to the post office to mopping the floors.

If you have several employees, you could collect all the DAILY ROUTINE CHECKLISTS, spread them out on a table, and quickly see who is doing what or who *needs* to do what.

*Systems are your eyes and ears!*

One way to start building the DAILY ROUTINE CHECKLISTS is to have everyone in your organization write down everything they do. And I mean *everything*. You will be greatly surprised at how much some people do and how little others do. You will also find some people are doing the same or overlapping tasks as another person, but at different times. This is an easy fix. Have one person do the task all the time, if possible. Remember: *Standardization*. You will see, with DAILY ROUTINE CHECKLISTS, how easy it is to get every task completed in your organization—*every day, every time, whether you're there or not!* Let me give you an example of how detailed our daily routine checklists have become:

## Keep the Music Playing

We had a cassette player (before the days of DVDs) that played music while callers were on hold. It would shut itself off every week or so. Well, I wanted it playing all the time, right? But I either had to *remember* to check it myself or put it on someone's DAILY ROUTINE CHECKLIST:

☐ Music on Hold Player is working

We did that, and it was checked every morning until we improved the system by purchasing a player that didn't shut off. Continual improvement at work!

This may seem to be a small thing, but several "small" things can often add up to big frustrations. Imagine having hundreds, to thousands of tasks getting done every time, every day, without your constant supervision. Your business starts to run like a super clean, well-oiled machine; and with these tasks being done automatically, you begin to notice a more peaceful atmosphere.

## QUALITY / SERVICE CONTROL CHECKLISTS

These types of checklists are crucial to any company that wants to guarantee quality and service. You may not be a manufacturer, but every company and organization has a product it is selling or promoting.

Your product may be a service, but it should be *quality* service.

I have been asked many times by service organizations why I think their business needs the same kind of QUALITY CONTROL CHECKLISTS as a manufacturer. Somehow they think they just need a *verbal* commitment to quality and service.

It doesn't matter how committed you are—without a checklist system, you cannot *guarantee* or *prove* quality or service, because you are human and you can't remember to complete every process consistently.

A company president I will tell you more about later in this book, said, "We don't need systems, we just need good people!" Think about that statement for a moment. Aren't you glad the airlines think differently? Before trained, professional pilots—no doubt *good people*—take off and land, they use a checklist. They know that all it takes is one time to forget to do something—like put down the wheels before landing—and many people will die.

After having a lot of success with checklists in my own company, I wondered why hospitals didn't have one person going down a simple checklist before a surgeon starts to operate. You have probably heard horror stories of the wrong leg being cut off, etc. Well, thank God, the better hospitals are now doing just that—checklists! Yes, the doctor is a trained professional, but he also has a million other things—and patients—to remember each day. With a checklist, it is almost impossible he will operate on the wrong leg.

### The Correct Way to Use a Checklist

When you use a checklist properly, the list of items/prompts on the checklist is to be completed *one prompt/item at a time*. When one item is completed, it is checked off as completed. Do not complete all the items on a checklist and *then* go down the list checking them off as "completed." By the same token, you don't check off everything on the checklist *first*, and then go about doing the tasks by memory. If you do that, you are gambling with the results. The checklist is used to focus your attention on one thing at a time.

Have you ever read something and it turns out later, you had read it wrong? Or, you were supposed to do something and it turns out you didn't, but you "just knew" you had? OK, so we're human, and we don't see or do things the same way every time. Our mind may be focusing on numerous things, or something major, and overlooking something small. The airline pilot could be focusing on the weather or passengers and miss a small light alerting him his landing gear is up or down.

**CHECKLISTS ARE NOT FOR "DUMMIES"**
but for busy, normal human beings
who simply can't remember
everything about everything all the time.
**Checklists make necessary details a
no-brainer!**

### First Day On The New Checklist System

True story. I have a fond memory of the first day we used the checklist system. There were a lot of skeptics and naysayers when we first began to develop the QUALITY CONTROL CHECKLIST SYSTEM. I wanted to start using them in the pressroom first. On day one, I walked out into the pressroom with the first checklist and gathered everyone in production around a table for a demonstration on how to use a checklist. I had the press operator set up a letterhead job and get it ready for approval. After he made ready his press, and printed the first letterhead sheet, he brought it to me to be approved, using the checklist. I took the new QUALITY CONTROL CHECKLIST, along with the DIGITAL JOB TICKET, which contained the specifications for printing the letterhead, and started down the checklist.

**The first item to check on the checklist was:**

☐ Ink color correct

I compared the color of ink on the letterhead with the ink that was specified on the DIGITAL JOB TICKET. It was correct. I made a check in the box by the item.

**Next item read:**

☐ Paper type correct

I compared the paper type of the letterhead with the paper type specified on the DIGITAL JOB TICKET and it also was correct. So I put a check by it.

**Next item read:**

☐ Paper color correct

The DIGITAL JOB TICKET specification was for a *gray color paper.* So I looked at the color of paper we were about to print—it was *cream color paper.* We had the *wrong* color paper, and we were about to print 10,000 letterheads incorrectly.

You should have seen the look on everyone's faces. Yes, the very first time we used a checklist it saved a job from having to be reprinted and having a very unhappy customer—not to mention the extra expense. I didn't have to convince anybody that using a checklist saved time. I believe it was providential, as we were starting out with our first QUALITY CONTROL CHECKLIST, and it worked. As a matter of fact, the person running the press that day became one of our strongest supporter of the checklist system. His rework, due to errors, almost went to zero. Thousands of dollars and hours have been saved using checklists. They can make the difference between success and failure in hard times, and were key to our success.

Some people welcome checklists, while others are insulted by them. Apparently, they believe they are just too smart to make a dumb mistake. But it happens to the best of us. No matter what anyone thinks about checklists—they work! It's been proven.

## Checklist Suggestions

Begin with the subject first, then the action verb, whenever possible. Example: Instead of a description that says:

❑ I took the mail to the post office

Better to use:

❑ Mail taken to post office

You don't need to use "I" in a checklist (e.g. "I did this" or "I did that"). Starting with the subject makes a checklist easier to read and follow.

## MASTER QUALITY CONTROL CHECKLIST

This one checklist contains all the necessary steps for the entire manufacturing or service process. We call the items on this checklist "prompts," because they direct us to check all process specifications to insure the job is error-free.

It starts with data entry and goes all the way through shipping and invoicing. You might call it the granddaddy of all quality control checklists. We sometimes refer to it as the "Driver Checklist," as it drives/manages our production quality control system step by step.

We developed this Master Control Checklist to be used in conjunction with our Job Jackets and Job Tickets. In most manufacturing facilities, the Job Jacket is used just to contain samples, proofs, purchase orders, or other job-related materials. It is also used to attach or hold the Job Ticket—the list of specifications, such as size, type, color, and other information needed to manufacture a job.

We use a 10x13 envelope as our Job Jacket, on both sides of which we print this Master Control Checklist. Since there is limited space on the envelope to print all the items needing to be checked for a process, an item/prompt may simply make reference to *another* process quality control checklist, printed on a separate sheet.

### Example of a Refereced Item on the Master Control Checklist

> ☐ Pressroom Quality Control Checklist (PD-543) has been completed, signed, stapled to a press sheet, and placed in Job Jacket.

*Note:* We also reference the document number of that other quality control checklist. We have found, the more places we can reference a system within another system, the more likely it will be used consistently and not get lost. See *Referencing* on page 46.

Remember, due to space constraints, as on our envelope, if a process is complicated and has many items that need to be checked, you should consider developing a separate checklist for that process, like the example above.

The MASTER CONTROL CHECKLIST SYSTEM is a great way to see at a glance that all Quality and Service Control Checklists have been completed without opening the Job Jacket and inspecting each of them. It is also a map or flowchart of your manufacturing or service process from beginning to end.

## POLICIES

Merriam-Webster defines a policy as *prudence in the conduct of affairs; a course of administrative actions.*

As I have already stated in this book, you must take the time, be prudent, and write things down so your employees don't have to guess what actions they should take, or not take, in various situations. We have used policies to exempt certain actions in certain situations. Instead of telling your employees to try to remember under which circumstances they should or should not do something, write it in a policy and it becomes part of the system.

When writing some policies, you don't always need to re-invent the wheel or start from scratch. There are many places to find written policies to give you a good starting point to customize them for your organization. You can find them on the Internet, especially Human Resources documents such as Employee Handbooks, etc.

A POLICY should reflect your MISSION STATEMENT and your CODE OF ETHICS. I strongly recommend you read them often.

There is also information on the Internet that will teach you how to write a policy, but if you use common sense, you should be able to write your own policies.

*Caution*: In your Employee Handbook, you need to be careful not to write anything that is unlawful. Also, be sure to mention somewhere in your handbook that the handbook itself is *not* a contract. Consult an attorney with any legal questions or other pitfalls in writing an employee handbook or other policies.

## PROCEDURES

I have really learned to appreciate written procedures as they are great time savers—and *time saved is money earned.* Written procedures also empower people to do their job with less direct supervision.

Think how many times an employee has come into your office to ask if you would show them *again* how to do a certain task. The employee says they forgot. But, why should he or she remember when they have you as a living, walking and talking computer/procedure? The employee uses the excuse, "Well, I don't do that task everyday and I just can't remember how to do it." So, you stop what you are doing and spend the time showing them *again* and *again* and *again*. Then when the employee finally gets it, they leave the company and you start over again, training the next person. This is where a good, time-saving procedure comes in. Take the time to write a procedure so anybody can follow it.

Remember we talked about *The General and the Private,* and how to "Roadie Proof" a system?

You will only have to write a procedure once and it becomes part of your OPERATIONS MANUAL. After writing the procedure, go through it step-by-step to find any holes while actually performing the task. Once you are satisfied you have found and corrected the holes, have someone else try the procedure, while you are watching to see if they stumble over any words, or if there is a missing step. Keep correcting and updating the procedure, until you know your employee can do it without any supervision.

The next time someone asks you *again* to show them how to do a task, simply hand them the procedure. Or, to really complete this system, the new procedure should be made accessible so they can find it themselves. Now, as you become more efficient at writing procedures, you can train others how to write them.

Can you see how you will profit by working ON your business?

> *The discipline of writing something down*
> *is the first step to making it happen.*
> Lee Iacocca

## ORIENTATION SYSTEM

A pressman we hired recently shared with me about a well-known printing company in our city where he had taken a job, and how excited he was to be hired. He heard they were one of the best printing companies around. After a few weeks he became very disillusioned; the things he had heard were not the things he was experiencing. They didn't give him an orientation, so he really didn't have a good picture of that company.

Organizations that do not have an ORIENTATION SYSTEM leave gaps in a new hire's knowledge of the company. It may take years of being employed there, before they really get a picture of the who, what, when, where and why of your company's operation.

We produced a two-hour orientation video, where I welcome a new employee, give an overview of our history, explain our QUALITY CONTROL SYSTEM and the 100 PERCENT SYSTEM OF CLEANLINESS; also, the POLICIES we consider crucial to our employees. The second part of the new hire orientation is facilitated by our Production Administrator, using a detailed Orientation Checklist and giving a test at the end. This is a super time saver.

When I first developed the ORIENTATION SYSTEM, it would take me three to four hours to facilitate *live* for new employees. Think how many hours I have saved over the years using video or DVD technology.

Every time we give an orientation, I hear from the new employee how grateful they are to know our history, our vision and a detailed explanation of our systems. They know who they are going to work for, what to expect, and what is expected of them.

A few years ago a friend of mine went to work for a national company, and I was asking him what the company was about and what his job entailed. I was amazed that even after several months he couldn't really explain their actual business, his job description or the company's mission. The company had few or no systems and management was apparently too busy *doing* to develop a detailed ORIENTATION SYSTEM.

New hires and each member of your team should be fully briefed on exactly what your company is about: the importance of your MISSION STATEMENT, a CHAIN OF COMMAND, what each department does and how they relate to each other; POLICIES and PROCEDURES, also the what and where of equipment, supplies and tools they will be using—*everything* they need to know to do their job.

A detailed ORIENTATION SYSTEM can make the difference whether your new employee hits the ground running, or flounders in confusion for a time trying to figure it all out for themselves.

# CHAPTER 11
# SYSTEMS THAT FOLLOW UP
# AND MEASURE IMPROVEMENT

## THE SYSTEM BUSTER

Any event in a business, that causes errors, mistakes, miscommunications, late deliveries, poor quality products, clutter from poor housekeeping, equipment failure, etc., is what we call a "System Buster."

We developed a unique tool that became the prime solution for transforming our company, which we simply call "The System Buster." A more accurate name for it would be "The System Buster Eliminator." It is a browser-based application designed to eliminate wasted resources in an organization, using the power of systems.

This solution detects, identifies, finds root causes, and stops system-busting/non-conforming events, permanently. The System Buster alerts management that a system—such as a checklist, policy, procedure or chain of command, etc.—is not being adhered to. It also alerts management to the absence of a needed system.

When someone fails to adhere to a system, it's like running a red traffic light and causing an accident.

Imagine the chaos and disorder on our city streets if we didn't have traffic lights and traffic cops. A traffic light is a system that keeps our vehicles from running into each other. How many times in business do we see people running into one another, because of overlapping duties? How many times have you observed mindless mistakes being made over and over, causing havoc and waste? The two main reasons for disorder in business are, a lack of good systems, and the failure of some to follow a current system.

Our company and many others have fixed thousands of system-busting events with the System Buster Eliminator. *Fix* is the key word here. It's not a bandage or temporary patch for a problem, but rather a permanent correction, so it doesn't happen again. When not dealing with dysfunction and disorder in your own organization, you have more time to serve your customers and grow your business.

The System Buster Eliminator is the most powerful management tool I have seen for bringing a business to order.

### Example of a System-Busting / Non-Conforming Event

Let's say my DAILY ROUTINE CHECKLIST has an entry with a check box to prompt me to be sure I have enough materials to do a certain job. If I ignore that prompt, but check it off as though I had done it, and later find out I do not have the needed materials, I have busted the system. In short, I lied! Consequently, the job has to be put on hold until the purchasing person can order and arrange for special pickup of the needed materials. This failure to adhere to the system has stopped production, cost the company time and money, and caused disorder—all because I was *non-conforming*.

Remember, a system is like a circuit on a circuit board. This *system-busting/non-conforming event* just shorted out the circuit — an example of one system affecting another system.

### Submitting a System Buster

When a *system-busting event* occurs, such as an error, the one who catches it submits a SYSTEM BUSTER to management stating only what happened. Management completes the SYSTEM BUSTER form by identifying the root cause and all who were involved in the error. In the example above, management would then enter the name of the person who failed to order supplies. Management then determines if it is a *personal error* or *system error*—the two main reasons anything goes wrong inside any totally-systematized organization.

**1. Personal Error**. This is where a person fails to follow the system, as in the previous example. The Administrator of the SYSTEM BUSTER system would then meet with the person to determine the root cause. The usual response is, "I was in a hurry, so I didn't follow the checklist properly." We remind the employee of the reasons we have checklists, and that checking off an item as completed, when it is *not*, is falsifying the checklist. We take this seriously, and when it occurs we let the employee know it's not acceptable. We have them sign the SYSTEM BUSTER form acknowledging a *personal error*. Then we move on.

If an employee gets multiple SYSTEM BUSTERS, due to *personal errors*, we may place copies in their employee file and fill out a disciplinary form. This is also reported in the employee's yearly Performance Evaluation. You will know right away if an employee is going to adhere to the system.

At this point, you may be thinking this all sounds a bit stringent, but that is not the intent. If you want to stop the chaos in your company, everyone needs to be accountable. We give grace when grace is due, and over the years we've only had to fill out a few disciplinary forms. When people realize we are committed to this continual improvement system, they will either embrace it or leave the organization. As you can see, the SYSTEM BUSTER is also an excellent *follow-up system* to all of your systems. When employees know your systems are followed up and followed through, you will find your employees more supportive and compliant.

**2. System Error**. This is an event, the remedy of which is not found on any CHECKLIST, PROCEDURE, POLICY or any written system. It was never incorporated into the system, because the event was never encountered before—or, if encountered, not properly addressed. Therefore, it is a *system error* and not a *personal error.*

### Predictable Event or Unpredictable Event

When the root cause of an event has been identified as a *system error*, management meets with those employees affected by the *system error* to find out whether it was a *predictable event* or an *unpredictable event*.

If found to be *predictable* and *preventable*, we brainstorm until we find a solution, and then incorporate it into the system to stop this error from recurring.

If the event is found to be *unpredictable*—it may be due to one of the following:

- **An Act of God** (e.g. lightning strikes your power grid causing you to miss a deadline).

- **A mistake made by your vendor or customer,** where they provided you with wrong information or materials.

On the SYSTEM BUSTER form there is a place to check *Vendor* or *Customer Error,* and enter their name. This information should go into a database, allowing you to pull a report as to how many times a vendor or customer has caused problems for your company.

Regarding vendors, these reports can be brought to their attention in the hopes they will fix *their* problems. If they *don't,* you can then make the decision about finding a new vendor. ISO companies track vendor errors to keep vendors accountable and compliant in the way they conduct business, and to maintain quality and service. In the ISO system, a vendor can actually be fined or dropped as a *preferred vendor.* See ISO, Chapter 20.

You can also pull a report on how many times a *customer* causes errors, so you can train or help your customer in providing you with correct information. Again, if they will not cooperate with you, you may find they are causing you too much grief. There are times when the customer is NOT always right!

The good news is, when the vendor or customer makes the mistake, they should pay for the cost of correcting it.

There is also a place on the SYSTEM BUSTER form to check an event as *undetermined* or an *Act of God.*

For *unpredictable events,* such as Acts of God, we have emergency or disaster recovery plans, and educational tools for our customers and vendors to help them reduce their own errors. You may want to give all of your customers and vendors a copy of this book or other books that might help them. Until I wrote my book, I used to buy and give away copies of *The E Myth* to my customers.

Now do you see how using the SYSTEM BUSTER can turn an organization into a powerful machine for delivering great quality and service? Your internal chaos can be almost totally eliminated.

THE SYSTEM BUSTER ELIMINATOR allows everyone in the company to be involved in correcting and improving the system. If someone fails to adhere to the system, and it bottlenecks another's workflow, then the person whose work is disrupted can submit a System Buster. They are helping to identify system busting/non-conforming events, so it can be fixed as a team.

The idea is not to place blame, or tattle on another employee, but for the purpose of continual improvement and fixing problems. Some will avoid submitting a System Buster thinking they may get someone in trouble with management. Others think this is like "Big Brother" in action.

This is where training and leadership comes in; by reminding your employees of the company's mission to give the customers great service and quality products. You need to share with your employees, that you want the best for them; that you are not looking to find fault with them, but looking for any faults in the system so you can fix them as a team.

## How Good is Good Enough?

A Customer Service Representative (I'll call her Martha) came into my office one day to go over some SYSTEM BUSTERS that identified her as the source of certain errors. She told me she was growing tired of signing these SYSTEM BUSTERS and thought we were "going too far." She had never worked for a company with a system that held her accountable to this extent. I said, "Martha, how far do you think we should go in trying to fix problems at our company? Do you think we should get 80 percent of the problems fixed and not worry about the rest?"

She said, "No!"

I said, "Well, what if we fix *90 percent* of the errors or problems? Would *that* be good enough, even though the 10 percent we don't fix affects the person in another department and makes their job more difficult?"

She said, "No!" Then, to my surprise, she said, "How about 98 percent?" But no sooner had she said it, she paused and said, "You can't! You can't stop at 98 percent! You have to try to fix everything!" She signed the SYSTEM BUSTERS without any more complaining.

## REWORK DUE TO ERROR REPORT

We have a report in the SYSTEM BUSTER system that is used to track how many reprints we have on jobs due to errors. When a SYSTEM BUSTER is issued and we determine we have to rework a job, we check a box called REWORK DUE TO ERROR. This enables us to pull a report on how many jobs had to be reworked in any given period. This allows us to measure/benchmark our success, or lack thereof, in the process of improving our production quality control systems.

We have been very successful in reducing our REWORK DUE TO ERRORS to less than one half of one percent; some months we have had *zero* errors. This will fluctuate from time to time. Whenever we notice these errors increasing outside an acceptable range, as the owner I get involved. We then hold a special meeting with those responsible, to remind them of the purpose and importance of our systems; also to encourage them not to continue this pattern.

### Perception Versus Reality

I was going over the Pressroom Performance Evaluations with our Production Administrator, and decided to do a little test. I asked her—out of all the press operators, which one did she *think* had the most rework due to errors? She told me Harry had the most and Tommy had the least. I thought her assumption was right, but it was just a gut feeling. So I asked her to pull a report of the REWORK DUE TO ERRORS in SYSTEM100™ for each operator, for a given period.

The report showed just the *opposite* of what we had both perceived. Actually, Tommy had the most reprints and Harry had the least. The reality was, the Production Administrator and I were both wrong. This is another reason why systems work, and why you should NOT trust *just y*our perceptions. Had we gone with our feelings we might have reprimanded or dismissed the wrong person.

An employee's rework, and the cost to the company, should be documented in their Performance Evaluation.

## A SYSTEM TO CHANGE THE SYSTEM

Yes, you also need a system to change the system! It is called a DOCUMENT CHANGE/UPDATE SYSTEM.

I will never forget the time I wanted to give up on this system stuff. It was the day one of my Customer Service Reps came into my office to tell me there had been an error on a job and the customer was not happy. So I asked what had happened to cause the error. When I was told, I was devastated. I said, "We had that error happen just last week and I *know* we fixed the system by updating the PRESS-ROOM QUALITY CONTROL CHECKLIST that addressed that error!" I rushed out to the pressroom and grabbed a checklist. The update I had personally made was not on it. I asked the pressman, "Where are the *new* checklists I gave you last week?"

He said, "I put the NEW checklists in the rack along with the OLD checklists, because I didn't want to waste paper."

Frustrated, I said, "You have to understand, when we update a checklist the old ones *must* be thrown away! Using an old checklist can cost hundreds or thousands of dollars and it's not worth saving a few pennies worth of paper."

*However, I realized it was not his fault—it was mine.*

W. Edwards Deming, of the famed Deming Application Prize for quality, believed that if you don't give your employees the right tools, and the time to do their job, then you shouldn't blame them for the results. A system is a tool.

I went back to my office feeling a bit discouraged, but it only lasted a few minutes and then the light bulb came on—we need a SYSTEM TO CHANGE THE SYSTEM.

I went to work building the checklist system for changing and updating our documents. One of the prompts on the checklist was:

> ☐ All copies of prior versions of this document have been discarded in every location.

Well, that fixed that problem, and we haven't had that issue show up again!

## Employee Performance Evaluations

At least once a year, management should provide a written Performance Evaluation to an employee—sort of like a school report card. This is a great way to benchmark their progress. Just as the company should be improving, so should every employee improve. It's also a good tool that allows owners or upper management to observe how supervisors evaluate people they supervise.

### Department Politics in Action

*Story time* . . . I asked one of my managers (I'll call him Mickey) to give an evaluation of the employees in his department. I went over each evaluation to get a sense of how he evaluated certain employees and, after signing off on them, I gave them to our Human Resources Department for filing.

About six months later, Mickey left on his vacation and while he was gone, I decided to fill in for him, to get a first-hand overview of his department. I believe it's a good idea for an owner to work in a department for a day or two, from time to time, to get a fresh vision for how the systems are working.

We had also just installed our new computerized Time Management System that reports how long it takes to do a specific task. I noticed an employee (let's call her Sally) seemed very slow in doing her main task. That was the impression I was getting—but, again, I've learned not to go by impressions or feelings alone.

So I did the right thing and pulled a detailed report of every job Sally had worked on for the past month. The report showed me she was taking almost twice as long as she should to do the job.

I discussed the matter with various people in the department and they all confirmed Sally was not only slacking, but reported other negative habits. I asked each of them if they had reported it to Mickey, the department supervisor. They *all* said they had. Some also told me in private, they were a little nervous about going over Mickey's head. I pulled Sally's latest Performance Evaluation to see how Mickey had evaluated her and was surprised to see Sally had been given very high marks in just about every area of her performance.

When Mickey returned from vacation I gave him a *written* report of everything I had witnessed in his absence, and what the employees under his supervision had shared with me. Mickey did not have a good explanation, other than to say the employees were wrong in their assessment of Sally. But the "system" said otherwise, and confirmed what her co-workers had reported.

After this incident, I implemented THE BUCK STOPS HERE SYSTEM (see page 113), as well as other follow-up systems, to help ensure this didn't happen again. As you can see, an evaluation is valuable in more ways than one.

> *Nearly all men can stand adversity, but if you want*
> *to test a man's character, give him power.*
> Abraham Lincoln

## TASKS/PROJECTS MANAGEMENT SYSTEM

To help with the transformation of your organization or business, you need a system for administering projects/tasks for your employees. A Task Management System enables you to oversee and watch an organization transforming before your very eyes, as various projects are completed.

This is where you can test the leadership skills and creativity of your employees—the cream of the crop will surface here. You are not spoon-feeding them completed instructions they simply follow—but rather, you are assigning them either a one-time project, such as overseeing the installation of a new copier, paint touchups; or maybe giving them a task to actually build a system (e.g. write a Policy or a Procedure). Like other systems, a Task Management System must have follow-up.

You could start your TASK MANAGEMENT SYSTEM with a simple list of projects in a spreadsheet or a task management application. There are many programs for you to choose from, one of which is our own SYSTEM100™ software, that has an excellent task system.

When an employee submits a suggestion for improvement using our SYSTEM100™ software, it immediately sends email notification to the administrator of the TASKS/PROJECTS MANAGEMENT SYSTEM. If the suggestion is approved for implementation, it is then categorized, prioritized and assigned as a task to a certain employee. We have a group of employees who volunteer to be a part of what we call our "Task Team."

Special tasks are assigned to these employees according to their individual skills, outside their normal job descriptions. When they finish their assigned task they check it off as *completed* in the SYSTEM100™ TASKS/PROJECTS SYSTEM. It automatically sends another email to the administrator who assigned the task, stating the task has been completed; whereby, the administrator can follow-up.

Using time-keeping software, our employees clock in on a process called SPECIAL TASKS/PROJECTS. The TASKS/PROJECTS administrator is able to track how much time we spend on these special projects for a given period. We can create a benchmark, a ratio of *chargeable* work versus *unchargeable* work. In this way, we can keep it in balance and, if needed, we can even create a budget for time spent on special projects.

You see, most companies have slow periods, but they don't always use the slowdowns effectively. They likely have no written list of improvements to be accomplished. Many suggestions for improvement have long been forgotten, and the rest are assigned off-the-cuff by the owner or supervisor, with little or no preparation or forethought.

I believe when a company or a department has a slowdown, the company should have ready a TASK/PROJECT SYSTEM. These tasks are not meant to be busy work; they should be tasks or projects that will help transform the company into one of excellence.

## TIME-KEEPING/FLOOR DATA COLLECTING SOFTWARE

I believe if you have four or more employees you should also strongly consider time-keeping/floor data collecting software, instead of using time clocks with time cards. Some floor data collecting software may be stand-alone or a module of a more complex MIS (Management Information Systems) software. Time-keeping software can readily be found on the Internet and will pay for itself—in some cases, in the first few months.

The first week we used our time-keeping software, I asked one of our supervisors if he had noticed anything different since we started the new system. He said he noticed workers were not going out to the smoking area as much. When we used conventional time cards, employees were sometimes not clocking in and out for all smoke breaks, and were taking more breaks than allotted.

When our time-keeping software was implemented, the Plant Supervisor could see from his desk's computer who was clocked in, and on which job they were working. When the employees knew we knew who was on break or at lunch, that behavior stopped immediately. If you have a lot of employees and they are taking longer or extra breaks, a lot of money and production time can be lost.

Time-keeping software is also used for tracking the *estimated time* and *actual time* it takes to do a task/job, which can be used for benchmarking and improving production times.

## CHART OF ACCOUNTS

The Chart of Accounts is a systematic listing of all accounts used by a company (e.g. office supplies, leases, repairs, payroll, rent, utilities, etc.). A Chart of Accounts is found in all accounting programs, such as QuickBooks.

The great thing about having your accounting program set up with a Chart of Accounts customized to YOUR business is, you can get a daily, weekly, monthly and yearly breakdown to see where every dollar goes. This is a *must* for every owner of a business. Many business owners allow their accountant to set up the Chart of Accounts—and handle *all* the accounting, for that matter. The problem with that is, the accountant tends to set it up his way, and not necessarily the best way to run your business effectively.

### Eyes for Your Business

A business associate who was advising me years ago, said, "Philip, you need to have eyes for your business!" He had learned a hard lesson from losing a couple of his own businesses, as he had never taken the time to understand the financial part of doing business, and didn't have his eyes on the numbers to make the right decisions. He told me I needed to set up my own Chart of Accounts. At that time (I'm almost embarrassed to tell you)—I didn't even know what a Chart of Accounts was.

He called our industry association and they provided us with a Chart of Accounts customized for our industry. He helped me understand and customize our accounting program's Chart of Accounts to match the one from our industry. Most trade associations have a standard Chart of Accounts established for their particular industry. If not, it's very easy to customize one for your own business.

From your Chart of Accounts you can then get the ratio of certain expenses, compared to your total sales for any period. You may be asking, "Why do I need this ratio and how can I use it?" You can compare/benchmark it with other companies in your industry to see if you may be spending too much money in certain areas. Or, you can compare/benchmark for budgets, etc.

## Chart of Accounts Saved Us Thousands

After the first month of using the customized Chart of Accounts to review our expenses, I could see how much I was spending on paper products—a very large expenditure for a printing company. I compared it with a Ratio Report published by our local trade association, listing all the printers in my area. It was broken down by profit leaders and all the rest of the printers, showing the ratio of expenditures on materials and labor, compared to total sales for the past year. I looked at the current year's Ratio Report and, to my amazement, found I was paying 10 percent more on paper than the profit leaders in my industry were paying. Well, immediately I called my paper representatives to meet with me and shared with them what I had discovered using the Industry Ratio Report. I was given an immediate 10 percent reduction in my cost of paper. That one Ratio Report saved me thousands of dollars! Would your accountant know if you were spending too much on a certain item compared to other companies in your industry? I would hope so!

As I learned from my business associate, "You should use your Chart of Accounts to give you those *eyes* for your business," because it gives you clearer vision for better decisions.

## INVENTORY SYSTEM

Every well-organized business needs to have an inventory of all of its assets broken down into different categories, like computer hardware, software, office furniture and decor, machines and tools, office supplies, and other consumables. Businesses lose a great deal of money through theft and misplaced assets and other materials.

The housekeeping of some companies and organizations is so poor, assets, machine parts and other materials are frequently being lost due to clutter and junk laying everywhere. In this type of environment you may buy two of everything—*one to use and one to lose.* It should be on someone's DAILY ROUTINE CHECKLIST to update and make sure all new assets and other new materials being purchased for the organization are being updated in the Inventory System. Inventory software can be found on the Internet at very affordable prices.

## BENCHMARKING—FOR MEASURING RESULTS

Benchmarking is a standard or ratio used for comparison.

The best way to offset skepticism is to measure your results to see if a system is working. Once you post the results so your employees can actually see them, they will be more receptive. Most people like to see how productive they are, and how the company is progressing. Remember how some of you were anxious to get your report card in school at the end of the six-week period? In the same way, *our* employees look forward to seeing our charts and reports at the end of the month. They actually challenge one another to do better. We have found which systems work by measuring to see if we are improving or not. We have taken down systems where results were minimal, and where running the system was not worth the cost.

For some, payroll can be the number one expense. Overstaffing sends many companies into bankruptcy. Benchmarking can help you know how much personnel you need.

*Example of how to figure Labor Ratio:*

Monthly Payroll Cost ($70,000) divided by Monthly Total Sales ($250,000), giving you a labor ratio/benchmark of 28 percent.

Find out how other profit-leading companies in your industry are doing, which will help you set some benchmark goals.

When your benchmarks at the end of a month show you're heading in the wrong direction, you can address the situation immediately. A lot of companies wait until they are in trouble, then call in an expensive consultant to find out what's wrong and, usually, by that time it's too late.

We have found—under normal economic conditions—with our *daily* approach to improving our systems, we get satisfactory-to-excellent benchmark reports.

# CHAPTER 12
# SALES AND MARKETING SYSTEMS

## SALES SYSTEM

Many companies have very few systems or controls for their Sales Department, other than hiring salespeople, showing them an office; then telling them to "get out there and sell something." Their main concern is a salesperson's total sales for a given period of time—but that alone does not give the owner or manager "eyes" to see what a salesperson is actually doing. Consequently, they miss the opportunity to help a salesperson become truly successful. A company can lose a great deal of money with this fly-by-the-seat-of-your-pants system.

There are some salespeople who stay with a company for a year or two, then move to the next company—stay there a year or two, and so on. These salespeople are aware most companies have no system for tracking their activities; they just receive a draw or salary and, essentially, have to answer to no one. It's almost a con game. I don't think they consider themselves dishonest people, but I believe if they were truly honest with themselves, they would have to admit they put in little effort to get sales and are not benefiting the company. On the other hand, if this same person worked for a company that had a good sales system, they would be more likely to flourish.

I have interviewed many salespeople and one of the questions I ask an applicant is, "Do you have a system for selling?" The answer is generally very vague, or they list a few things they do to make a new sale—none of which, in my estimation, would make them very productive or consistent in selling.

## No System for Selling

I remember a sales interview with a young woman who had just left a company that had recently declared bankruptcy. When I asked her about her system of selling she said she really didn't have a system and had never been asked to adhere to one. I sensed she wasn't all that passionate about sales as a profession, as much as she was just looking for a job. Apparently, she had been selling for a while, going from one company to another, never achieving any real success. When she asked me about the pay, I said, "Before we talk about pay, I want to know about your sales." After discussing her former sales figures, and what she wanted to be paid, it didn't even approach the ratio needed to compensate her. She informed me, however, she had several companies competing for her services. I explained our Sales System to her; that it would track her calls, appointments and other activities, and she would also need to turn in a DAILY ROUTINE CHECKLIST.

She never called back, and we probably saved a lot of money.

Yes, you can and will lose money on some salespeople, even with a system. The good news about a system is, you don't have to lose money for a year or two before realizing a person is not going to work out.

When you put someone on a *system* of selling you can tell fairly soon if they are right for the job. At times we have kept some salespeople longer than we should, based on their performance; however, overall, our system of selling has saved unnecessary expense, and helped some salespeople to rethink their *own* method of selling.

## Sales Benchmarking

I think it is obvious a company should be tracking the salesperson's sales in dollars. However, in a good sales system you should also track the amount of suspect, prospect, and customer calls made each day, as well as the number of appointments made with prospects. All this data should be placed into a graph to benchmark the results. You will be surprised at how a simple system like this will give you a clearer vision for your Sales Department, even with one salesperson.

If a salesperson says they will work for commission only, then you know this person is serious about selling. They know selling on straight commission, if it's a fair percentage, is the path to great money and they don't need you to hold their hand. If they sell, they make money and you make money. If they don't, you pay nothing. In that situation, you may not require them to follow your sales system—however, they must follow other company systems (e.g. a Daily Routine Checklist, Estimate Checklist, Order Entry Checklist, etc.). In one way this type of salesperson is like contract labor—not much fuss!

I believe, however, all salespeople should want a strict system of selling, and should be constantly looking for ways to improve their sales system.

A good system, just as in production or service, is the key to growing a great Sales Department. You should have benchmark charts to show progress. Your sales team can actually have fun using these benchmarks as they challenge one another and brainstorm how to bring in new customers.

*Be diligent to know the state of your flocks*
*and attend to your herds.*
Solomon the Wise

## MARKETING SYSTEM

Not long ago, one of my sales people sent me a resignation letter that made me stop and reconsider ALL of our Sales and Marketing methods. To say the least, I was taken all the way back to the day I decided to systematize my entire production and service for our company.

This person was a new hire who had come to the conclusion that *cold calling* was not her cup of tea. The letter was direct and well thought out. It told me how much she appreciated our company and all I had tried to do to help with her sales effort. It also stated our company was the most organized, in fact, the most "stellar" company she had ever worked for, "BUT," she went on to say. . .

"Philip, I believe you need to put the same effort and creativity into your Sales and Marketing as you did with building your Operations Manual and SYSTEM100™." She also said, what we did NOT have was a good marketing plan, and we needed to have buyers *opt-in to us*, rather than *us cold-calling them*.

I had to admit she was right! Ours was a shoot-from-the-hip, shotgun approach to marketing. The truth hurt. I had systems for tracking sales people at that time, but we had no definitive plans or written systems for marketing.

Well, it was decision time again for me. I was the problem—I knew I would always be the problem, until I changed. I closed my office door and began to consider how we could market systematically. I found myself saying out loud, "Automatic marketing." That sounded good! Surely, someone must have thought of automatic marketing already—maybe even written on the subject. And sure enough, someone had! I found a book by Benjamin Hart and, wouldn't you know, the title was *Automatic Marketing*.

Since reading Hart's book, I have been on a quest to use some of his suggestions, and those of other writers on the subject. Due to the fact that, we have been building systems to run our company for many years, it was easy enough for us to write automatic marketing techniques into our system.

By using several of our existing systems—DAILY ROUTINE CHECKLIST, PROCEDURES, the SYSTEM100™ TASK SYSTEM and other programmed solutions—we began building the AUTOMATIC MARKETING SYSTEM for our company. By reviewing our employees' DAILY ROUTINE CHECKLISTS, we decided who would be best suited for the various jobs that needed to be done on our new AUTOMATIC MARKETING SYSTEM.

We have implemented many marketing ideas by putting them into a written system. Here is one example:

## Customer and Prospect Information System

Your database of customers is the most valuable asset you have for marketing your business. You need to keep it cleaned/purged and updated consistently, just like other documents in your OPERATIONS

MANUAL. You could operate like most companies: when the feeling hits them, they have someone try to clean up the database. But, you can guess how that goes—lost numbers, names, and other information. Again, you need a system for updating your customer and prospect information, so you're not playing *Russian Roulette* with your database. You need to have a *checklist*, so all information is correct: name, address, type of business, products used, etc.

We have prompts on our ESTIMATING CHECKLIST and JOB ENTRY CHECKLIST, along with a written procedure for entering customer and prospect information in our database.

## Automatic Marketing Systems

1. Direct Mail Marketing System—Postcards and letters are mailed systematically by using prompts on DAILY ROUTINE CHECKLISTS.
2. Automatic Responders—A customized, online program used to communicate with customer/prospect (e.g. thank you for your order, special holiday or repeat customer discounts and gifts, etc.) by retrieving certain records from our database.
3. Survey System—Customer feedback on our quality and service is collected using the Automatic Responder System, and through direct calling by our Customer Service Personnel using prompts on their DAILY ROUTINE CHECKLISTS.
4. Referral System—For referrals, we offer discount coupons to customers through the online Automatic Responder System, and printed coupons for sales people.
5. Discount Coupon System—This customized program is used to create coupons and to track usage.
6. Request Sample System—Customers can request samples of our work and obtain discount coupons from our Website.
7. Request Custom Quote System—From our Website.
8. Help Tools on our Website—For aiding customers (Templates, FAQs, etc.)
9. Website Optimization System—This is the process by which we improve the volume and quality of traffic to our Website from search engines, through reciprocal links, paid search engine ads, and continual improvement of our Website content. We also use

analytical tools to automatically track Web traffic and determine to which pages visitors are attracted.

10. <u>Endorsement System</u>—Customer endorsements are posted on our Website using a prompt on DAILY ROUTINE CHECKLISTS.

11. <u>Magazine Ads</u>—These are placed on a recurring basis in select magazines to promote our Company Name, Website URL, and '800' Number; also to announce Special Offers.

As with all other areas of your business, without an effective written system for marketing, you will *never* have consistent, measurable results!

## CHAPTER 13
## A SYSTEM OF CLEANING

### THE 100 PERCENT SYSTEM OF CLEANLINESS

Don't miss this! *If you don't get anything else out of this book, get this!* THE 100 PERCENT SYSTEM OF CLEANLINESS is the most surprising system I discovered on my journey to bringing my business to order. It is used to clean and organize all of our *hard* systems—things like machinery, cabinets, desks, the entire building and grounds, etc. With this system, we have received more attention and positive feedback than any other system we have implemented. The reason is, people get a lasting impression of your business when they see it for the first time.

### Truth . . .

*You don't get a second chance to make a first impression!*

People have a preconceived picture in their mind of what a printing company looks like. So, when they see our offices, bindery, pressroom and warehouse are immaculately clean, it takes them by complete surprise. They expect to see dirty floors with ink stains and paper lying everywhere. We keep our company clean for the same reason people dress up to make a good first impression. Your house cleaning is out in the open and cannot be hidden. It's an open statement of who you are. Simply put, the 100 PERCENT SYSTEM OF CLEANLINESS is: Everything in its place and a place for every thing.

### The 100 Percent System of Cleanliness in Action

Several years ago, our Production Manager was very frustrated with Mark Campolo, one of my most dedicated employees, about his messy work area. I've asked his permission to use his real name. Mark has always been hardworking and very cooperative, but when it came to keeping his work area clean, he was about a two on a scale of one to ten. Our Production Manager had come to the point of wanting to fire Mark, and that made me very uncomfortable. I liked Mark, so I asked the Production Manager to give me time to work with him and to develop a system of cleaning just for him.

As Dr. W. Edward Deming believed, I also believe: *If you don't have a system/tool for performing a task, then you shouldn't expect people to perform at top levels.* Although we kept a fairly clean facility before we discovered this system, it was nowhere near "world class"—and that was and is the mission.

I asked Mark to come into work the following Saturday and Sunday. I told him he and I would do a detailed cleaning, and develop a cleaning system for his small press department. Before Saturday arrived, I purchased special hard steel cabinets, several cases of plastic bins, and a variety of other organizational supplies; we already had a great label printer.

We started out early Saturday morning cleaning and organizing. We wanted a *designated* and *labeled* location for every single item in his department. But, each item wasn't going to be located just anywhere—it would be in a well-thought-out and planned location. It had to be convenient. Everything needed to be in an easy-to-clean, permanent and sturdy container (no cardboard). And the container had to look good. We cleaned and scrubbed all day Saturday, then again after church on Sunday. By Monday morning, we had his department looking great.

With each item to be organized, I would ask Mark questions like, "Do you use this item on a daily basis? Occasionally? Or does this item even belong in your department?" Let me tell you, it took about 120 total man-hours to completely develop this system. I had never cleaned and organized anything in my life to that degree of detail. We were extremely proud of it, so I decided to play a little game.

I asked one of the women in Customer Service to give Mark and me an inspection. I asked her to see if she could find anything, and I mean *anything* that was out of place, no matter how small or seemingly unimportant. I gave her the ground rules—I told her *every item* had a designated location that should be clearly labeled, and it should be in a permanent container that looked good. Well, she did her inspection and, being a detailed person, she found a plastic bin that wasn't labeled and one paper clip lying behind a work table. Yes, one paper clip. That's the kind of inspection I was looking for. So I labeled the bin, found the place where the other paper clips were located, and put the one paper clip in its place.

I heard comments from some employees, including the Production Manager, like, "Yeah, but will it stay clean?" To tell you the truth, I wasn't really sure.

I explained to Mark that, at the end of his workday, all he needed to do was put *all* the items he used back in their designated location, just as if he was filing papers. I asked him to notify me after he put everything up for the day and I would do an inspection. At the end of the day I inspected his department and it looked great. I did notice a T-square lying across the work table and some paper strips lying on top of the old plate camera. I also noticed a few small tools that were not in what we had agreed would be their designated location.

I said, "Mark, the T-square has a hook for you to hang it on— and it's labeled T-SQUARE."

He said, "Oh, yeah." And he hung it up.

Then I looked around and said, "What are all those paper strips on your work table?" He said he used them for masking out certain images on the camera.

I also asked, "Why are these small tools not in their designated location?"

He said, "Well, when I started working I realized they weren't in a very handy place."

So right then, together, we found a more convenient location for the tools he had moved. I got a plastic tray and labeled it MASKING SHEETS for those loose strips of paper. The next day we repeated the inspection process and very few adjustments were made to our new cleaning system. The following day I went out for my inspection and his department was at, what I call, "100 percent"—every item, down to a paper clip, was in its designated location. Wow!

From then on, Mark's department stayed between 98 and 100 percent. I can't tell you how proud and amazed I was at this discovery and how simple it was.

One day after Mark had gone home, I asked the Production Manager—who had wanted to let Mark go—and our Pressroom Supervisor, to come and see the Small Press Department. I asked them this question: If they had walked into this department and didn't know the person who was working here—on a scale of one to ten, as far as cleanliness and organization is concerned, what would they rate that person? They both agreed, "A nine or a ten." But, I said, "Since you know Mark, what is his rating, really? They both agreed, "A two or a three." You see, with a good system—a *two* became a *nine or ten*.

Since then, we have put the 100 PERCENT SYSTEM OF CLEANLINESS to work at every desk, every department, and in every area of our company. Again, we are following our MISSION STATEMENT of adhering to a system of cleanliness.

With the 100 PERCENT SYSTEM OF CLEANLINESS in place, if an item is out of its designated location, it sticks out like a sore thumb. It is very easy to do an inspection. In fact, as soon as you walk into a room you can see an item out of place. This makes managing easy—for example, if you have a room that is perfectly in order, and someone has left an old beverage can sitting out in the middle of it, you would notice it right away—but if you have the same beverage can sitting in a room full of clutter you might not notice it at all.

## Why the 100 Percent System of Cleanliness Works

Let's say we started the day with our workstation or desk somewhat in order. As the day goes along, we use more and more of our work materials and our workstation or desk becomes more cluttered. I'm sure you've seen people's workstation or desk looking like someone took a trash can and emptied it on top. You've seen whole departments looking as if a bomb had gone off in them. Chaos!

So when we can't stand the mess anymore we begin to straighten things up a bit, placing a stack of stuff here and a stack of papers there. This may look better—it may *look* clean and organized—but this is not a *system* of organization. This is just straightening up, because the next day when you straighten up, some items may be in a totally different place.

You may say, "Why does this matter?"

Well, it matters, because if you don't know where every item is, especially when you're using many items, a person who needs to work in your area *behind* you may take hours for them to find needed materials. Everyone should be able to find every item in your work area, effortlessly—especially you! Everyone should know exactly where the scissors are—not probably, but *exactly* where everything should be—because it is labeled and has a designated location. Sometimes you may even have one plastic bin for just one item, such as a flashlight. You may think this is overkill, unless you are the one doing the looking!

How many times have you gone looking for something as simple as a flashlight, and it took an hour or more to find it? Or, you lost several minutes looking for a file or a certain piece of paper, finally finding it in the clutter. The closer an area gets to 100 percent, the better it works, and the more time and money saved. To take it a little further...

The main principle of the 100 Percent System of CLEANLINESS is that *every* item has a designated and labeled location; and *every* item should be in its place. So, if 80 percent of your items have a place, and 20 percent do not have a place, you could call this an 80 percent system.

You say, "But, there are only a few items that don't have a des-ignated location—so what's the big deal?"

Ah, but if you *only* had an 80 percent system—after a while, some of the 80 percent starts getting lost in the 20 percent and vice-versa! The system begins to break down into chaos. That's why 100 percent works every time, day after day, month after month—*but any system less than 100 percent will start to break down.*

Can you imagine an engineer saying, "As long as 80 percent of the circuits are in place your television or computer should work just fine"? No, it works *just fine* because 100 percent of the circuits are in place.

Another great thing about this cleaning system is, *you only have to build it once*—as long as you get it to 100 percent—and then all you have to do is fine-tune it every now and then.

Do you see how this cleaning system works like the other systems mentioned in this book? They must be 100 percent—no gaps!

### Benefits of the 100 Percent System of Cleanliness

Let's talk money. You've heard "time is money!" Imagine you had a big glass fish bowl. Now, every time you or someone in your organization looked for something and couldn't find it, you noted on a small piece of paper the time it took to locate the item and how much money that time had cost. Then you placed these pieces of paper in the fish bowl. After a year, how full do you think that bowl would be? We have saved bowls and bowls of minutes and hours of time over the past many years, using the 100 PERCENT SYSTEM OF CLEANLINESS—not to mention the bowls of hours saved with the other cost-saving systems described in this book.

Another benefit is—when our outside cleaning service comes to vacuum, sweep, dust, mop, etc., at the end of the day, they don't have to straighten up and move everything out of the way before they begin cleaning. More time and money saved—and they can do what they do best, clean your business.

Our outside cleaning service is a very important part of our system, because they participate in the improvement of our company. They see how seriously we take the cleaning system. That's their business, and they appreciate being part of a business that understands *their* business. We have become a model place for them.

The 100 PERCENT SYSTEM OF CLEANLINESS is also a key component of our sales and marketing efforts. We have won over many potential clients just with a single tour of our facility.

Think about it—you may not need to hire that extra salesperson. You may just need to implement the 100 PERCENT SYSTEM OF CLEANLINESS.

A key benefit for me and our employees is coming into work each day: the floors are immaculate, and everything is in its place, no clutter, and no confusion, which means less stress and more pride in our work.

## Do We Just Clean All Day?

A new pressman we really wanted to hire came in to be interviewed and was shown around our plant. He remarked about it being the cleanest pressroom he had ever seen, and accepted the job the next day. However, later he related to me, he had gone home to talk it over with his wife and told her how clean everything was. He told her he was a little worried because he thought, to be that clean we must not have much work, so he guessed we just clean all day. Nothing could have been further from the truth!

Our press operators spend little time cleaning the pressroom. With the 100 PERCENT SYSTEM OF CLEANLINESS there is little to do except put the items you worked with that day back in their designated location. And most items are already in their place, because the location is so convenient you naturally put them there as you're working.

Our cleaning service sweeps and mops our pressroom floor every night, and they dust and wipe down the stainless steel workbenches. In most plants there is so much clutter, managers don't want outside cleaning services touching anything for fear of losing or ruining something.

The pressman I mentioned above told me later, how he had shown his daughters our pressroom and the presses he operated. He said this was the only company he had worked for where he felt proud to show his family. He went on to say, "Quite frankly, I had been ashamed to show them the other companies where I worked."

To me that one testimony is worth it all!

## OSHA v. The 100 Percent System of Cleanliness

I finally rushed from my office late morning, one October 31st. I was half way home and looking forward to helping my wife prepare for my son Paul's birthday party, when I received the call on my mobile phone. It was my office calling, informing me an OSHA inspector had arrived at our company and I had only thirty minutes to come back, or they would start the inspection without me. OSHA—the Occupational Health and Safety Administration—had made an unscheduled visit to inspect our facility.

"You're joking!" I responded to Jennifer, my Production Administrator. She assured me it was no joke. Jennifer was right in the middle of improving some of our health and safety systems—we had even discussed getting ready for a possible surprise OSHA inspection. "Wouldn't you just know OSHA would show up on Halloween!" I grumbled, as I called my wife Susan to tell her I would be late. Reluctantly, I hurried back to the office.

On the way, I remembered a recent conversation with a friend who also owns a printing company. He had just had a surprise inspection by OSHA himself, and had called to warn me it might happen to us anytime. He likened the experience to the Nazi Gestapo entering his building—flashing badges, interrogating his staff, and striking fear in his own heart that they might fine him heavily or even shut his business down. I had taken my friend's prompting to heart and decided to review our systems related to OSHA.

The drive back to my office allowed me to do a mental inventory of the things I was sure would pass inspection, but I dreaded what might turn out to be a lengthy inquest about things even our systems had missed. Fortunately, my wife and I had just seen a great film called *Facing The Giants,* and I was encouraged that my company had been prepared well enough that maybe even the "Gestapo" could not fault us now.

I began to relax and regain my confidence. I was thankful we had already made many improvements in safety and health issues. Due to our 100 PERCENT SYSTEM OF CLEANLINESS, we had everything organized, labeled, and in its place. Our employees had submitted countless suggestions for improvements over the years, due to our TQM CONTINUAL IMPROVEMENT SYSTEM. We had an organized "Right to Know" station set up with all of our MSDS (Materials Safety Data Sheets) documents and posters, along with our TAGOUT LOCKOUT SYSTEM.

Safety equipment (disposable ear plugs, back braces, etc.) was all in designated locations. Chemicals were stored in clean, labeled, heavy steel storage bins. This had been part of our system for years—and we continually *improve* that system, I reminded myself.

Jennifer had recently scheduled a training session with a local fire extinguisher company to give our staff training on how to use our fire extinguishers. It had occurred to me I had never actually had to pull the pin and fire one. Good chance to learn!

We had also scheduled training for the forklift. All of this, prior to OSHA's visit.

Arriving at the office, finally, I found Jennifer already in conversation with the inspector in our conference room. The atmosphere was pleasant enough and they were getting along nicely.

I was proud of how Jennifer handled herself; not only because she's my daughter-in-law, but because I can always be confident that we are on top of things with our systems. Of course, we didn't know exactly what would happen in this case, but our systems allow us always to be pro-active.

The OSHA inspector interviewed me first. He had his own checklist of questions we were able to answer without concern. One question—"Do your employees have access to OSHA's required documents?"—prompted a resounding (and relieved) "YES!" from me.

"We have a browser-based software system called SYSTEM100™ that gives our employees access to *all* documents and information needed to do a good job," I assured him, "along with information for their health and safety that OSHA requires." It's SYSTEM100™ that empowers our employees, enabling us to continually improve the company in all areas.

After touring and inspecting our plant, he described our house-keeping as "impeccable," and said it would go a long way in his report. I was able to appreciate the OSHA inspector's visit after all. Before he left, he thanked me and said, "Do you know how many companies I visit and I don't even know where to start, because there is so much clutter and chaos? It's nice to visit a company that really seems to GET IT!"

### Recap the 100 Percent System of Cleanliness

Every item has a designated and labeled location. Not 80 per-cent, but 100 percent of all items used. Also, every item should be in a permanent type of container, i.e. plastic bins, metal cabinets—not a cardboard box. At the end of the shift or day, all items are to be returned to their location.

It sounds simple, and it really is. However, most companies—especially manufacturing companies—are usually not very clean and organized, due to the simple fact they really don't have a *system of cleaning*. They may straighten things up and some may even have a maintenance crew to "clean" the offices, but I'm talking about a sustainable system that covers every area of the organization—*every* department, *every* desk, *every* cabinet, *every* machine, *every* table.

Not one thing is unaccounted for in the 100 PERCENT SYSTEM OF CLEANLINESS!

# CHAPTER 14
# PRODUCTION SCHEDULING SYSTEM

I'VE HAD MANY CONVERSATIONS with business owners and managers from all over the country about Scheduling Systems for projects, production and service. I've been asked many times, "How do you deliver product on time, every time at your company?" They expressed their doubts it could be accomplished at their own company, due to the difference between *their* turnaround times and ours, and the different types of product or service we each provide.

Well, I understand what they are saying, but at some point we must stop trying to look for reasons why things won't work and look for solutions to ensure they do.

Personally, I believe you should not promise to deliver product on a specific day if you can't *prove* the accuracy of your promise, based on prior benchmarks. That is, of course, unless you want to maintain the SYSTEM OF APOLOGY, and hire staff to make excuses for not delivering on time. I think you might just continue to stick to semi-promises like, "We'll give it our best shot," or "Well, if we're not too busy," or my personal favorite, "If the good Lord's willin' and the creek don't rise!"

I know the frustration of being told, "Your product will not arrive as promised," and then being given some lame excuse as to *why*—with a big ole "I'm sorry" at the end. How about a little *truth* with your SYSTEM OF APOLOGY!

I wrote an article for our online newsletter, *The Organizer,* titled "Printers Are Big Fat Liars." Unfortunately, it's not only printers. Many types of businesses and organizations can be "big fat liars" when it comes to delivering on a promise. Oh, I'm sure they don't purposely lie; however, some may stretch the truth so often it becomes their M.O. or normal way of doing business—and their excuse is, "Everybody does it!"

## Scheduling 101

To start, I would like to remind you again, as with any process or event that needs to happen in a consistent manner, and on a given date, you must have a *complete system—no gaps*.

To build a great Production or Service Scheduling System you need several systems working in concert for a complete solution, starting with a detailed map of the entire process, from start to finish.

Hereafter, the term "production" will be used to describe the steps or stages of a process, whether in service or manufacturing. The same basics apply whether you are a manufacturer, a food provider, a medical facility, service company, or a pig farmer.

There are many types of Production, Project and Service Scheduling software on the market. Some companies use industry-specific software, called MIS (Management Information Systems) or Excel spreadsheets; while others still use a manual scheduling board to show all the WIP (Work in Progress) for a given day.

These can be very helpful tools; however, they are still only part of the solution for building a great scheduling system.

As a job/project progresses through the production or fulfillment cycle, toward the due date, it moves from one process or work center to the next. These centers are the locations where the work/process is performed (e.g. planning, designing, data entry, printing/copying, proofing, assembly, labeling, recording, shipping, etc.)

A work center may involve several processes—like a group of similar machines, sometimes called *cost centers*. They can also be grouped into higher-level departments (e.g. Engineering, Production, Customer Service, Accounting, Shipping, etc.). Each process needs a quality control checklist to ensure a job/project is done right the first time, which is crucial to on-time delivery.

In commercial printing, a job travels through the production process starting at Data Entry and ending at Shipping. The time it takes a job to complete this production cycle is called *turnaround*.

*Example of a five-day turnaround of a job, cycling through work centers in the Printing Industry:*

1st Day—Data Entry and Proofing

2nd Day—Plating and Printing Press

3rd Day—Paper Cutting Machine

4th Day—Folding, Binding, etc.

5th Day—Shipping or Delivery

## Schedule Busters

A large company may have one or more employees whose sole job is manning the SCHEDULING SYSTEM.

The Scheduler normally receives his orders or updates from the Project/Production Manager who is generally running around the building putting out fires, trying to keep the wheels of production moving by directing and pushing jobs or projects from one work center to the next.

Management and Sales people pressure the Project/Production Manager when their jobs are running late, or they need to push through a "rush job" for their top client or customer. With some management or sales people, it seems *every* job is a rush job. They assume most of the jobs in progress are already late, and figure they need to pad or even fib about the due date to ensure it is going to be on time. This creates more pressure, chaos and lost production time.

The boss sometimes gets in on the act, barking orders to the Scheduler and Project/Production Manager, as he may have his own clients—and everyone knows the boss' jobs go through production, no matter what. He may also have a salesperson he's afraid of losing, breathing down his neck, reminding the boss she is the "top sales person" and her jobs are "priority one."

Common schedule busters are data entry errors. These data entry errors cause production slowdowns, while one department has to call and interrupt other departments to find the missing information or data. This is another major reason for REWORK DUE TO ERRORS. These errors are made for the simple reason, there's not a CONTROL CHECKLIST in place for entering data to create a JOB/PROJECT TICKET containing all specifications for production. The errors come from customers, sales people, customer service representatives, etc., not having correct information, leaving out certain information or inputting the information incorrectly.

To stop these schedule busters, we implemented the MASTER CONTROL CHECKLIST, along with an ESTIMATE/ORDER CHECKLIST. These detailed CHECKLISTS have eliminated 99.9 percent of all data entry errors—and reduced our overall waste by 70 percent.

To add more pressure and chaos to the schedule, an upset client or customer may call to report an error or desired change on his job, and to demand it be done or redone "RIGHT NOW." Now it's panic time. The entire process is moved around in order to accommodate this customer, at breakneck speed.

You know the old saying, "There's always enough time to redo a job, but never enough time to do it right the first time."

Worse case scenario: the unexpected seems to happen just when the production pressure is at its peak, and a key machine or work center breaks down. Now the whole production process goes into a tailspin.

A lot of breakdowns in equipment are due to the fact, there's not a well-planned PREVENTATIVE MAINTENANCE SYSTEM and a REPAIR REQUEST SYSTEM in place.

Due to the lack of a good PURCHASING SYSTEM, needed materials are not available or haven't been ordered when it's time to produce a job or project, causing delays. This could be a vendor error, or someone forgetting to order needed materials.

In some companies schedules are delayed or moved for the simple reason that certain employees object to or refuse to work overtime, even in the most urgent situations. Companies should have a written policy about working overtime—a policy that should be given to the employees as part of their orientation when they are first hired. At our company, the new employee signs the OVERTIME POLICY before being hired.

Still other companies allow their employees to consistently come to work late, or take leave without proper notification to management. We use the ABSENTEEISM SYSTEM and the REQUEST FOR LEAVE SYSTEM in our SYSTEM100™ software, which tracks and enables us to be proactive with our employees. This is to ensure we have consistent start times for production, and enough man hours to handle the production schedule. All vacations and requested leaves are posted on our COMPANY CALENDAR.

Another reason some schedules may be shifted around is, a company does not have TIME KEEPING/FLOOR DATA COLLECTING software that reports on *Actual Time* versus *Estimated Time* on a project or job (the estimated or actual time it takes for a job or project to go through the entire process, from start to finish. The company may never have measured, benchmarked, adjusted, and then repeated these steps, until they have a very close *Estimated Time* for how long each process in the production/project cycle takes to complete. Therefore, they really don't know the real turnaround time of a job, which makes the schedule a "guesstimate" at best. The *Actual Time* can only be measured after the work is completed, and then it should be used to benchmark for improvement. For any new process introduced in the production cycle a time study should be conducted to benchmark for an *Estimated Time*.

In many cases the Project/Production Manager is also the Scheduler and spends a lot of time trying to keep the schedule accurate, while fire-fighting in production.

As you can see, trying to please everyone while handling the schedule—along with many *system-busting/non-conforming events*—can be very challenging.

In most cases the Schedule Reports are not up-to-date; therefore, they are practically unusable. The reason these reports are sketchy is, by the time the Project/Production Manager sits down and inputs all the jobs/projects into the schedule, new work or rush jobs are being added to production automatically by online ordering, or Customer Service.

Also, there may have been a slowdown—a bottleneck—in production at a particular work center, that is not reflected in the production schedule.

So, on and on it goes! This is why many mid-sized to large companies have one or more persons overseeing and updating the schedule at all times.

When we began to implement our SCHEDULING SYSTEM, I had flashbacks of all the conversations I'd had with many vendors of MIS (Management Information Systems). Several of them, when demonstrating their software, honestly confessed that very few companies used their scheduling modules. They explained to me they were working on updates to fix the issues that companies had been complaining about. Some vendors claimed it was more likely a company's ill-use of their software, while other software companies claimed to be developing so-called "automatic" schedulers.

What I observed immediately, implementing the scheduling module of our MIS program was that, to guarantee on-time shipping, it would involve many of our current systems coming together in-concert to "complete the circle"—a SCHEDULING SYSTEM with no gaps.

*Let's review* the problems that cause chaos in a SCHEDULING SYSTEM:

**Problem:** Data Entry errors.
**Solution:** DATA ENTRY CONTROL CHECKLIST, MASTER QUALITY CONTROL CHECKLIST and an ESTIMATE/ORDER ENTRY CHECKLIST.

**Problem:** Too many hands in the pot—Sales Persons, Owner etc. demanding their jobs take precedent.
**Solution:** Know your capacity by having a system for benchmarking production times with TIME-KEEPING/FLOOR DATA COLLECTING software. Have a CHAIN OF COMMAND POLICY, who makes the decision about scheduling priorities.

**Problem:** Employees showing up late, at different times, or absent.
**Solution:** STARTING TIME POLICY for various departments, ABSENTEEISM POLICY, ABSENTEEISM REPORTING SYSTEM, REQUEST FOR LEAVE SYSTEM, COMPANY CALENDAR showing who will be out on certain days, and TIME-KEEPING/FLOOR DATA COLLECTING software.

**Problem:** Workers objecting or refusing to work overtime unless it is convenient for them.
**Solution:** OVERTIME POLICY, which is signed by the employee.

**Problem:** Rework due to errors.
**Solution:** QUALITY CONTROL CHECKLIST at each work center, to reduce errors. SYSTEM BUSTER SYSTEM, to locate and eliminate errors through systemization, so they don't happen again; also, to benchmark progress.

**Problem:** Client/Customer has changes to their job while still expecting their original due dates to be met.
**Solution:** A SCHEDULING POLICY, including an explanation of rush fees, due to customer changes or requests for quicker turnaround, is given to client/customer prior to start of job/project.

**Problem:** Necessary materials for production not available when it's time to start a process.
**Solution:** MATERIAL REQUISITION SYSTEM, PURCHASE ORDER SYSTEM, DAILY ROUTINE CHECKLIST, the 100 PERCENT SYSTEM OF CLEAN-LINESS, INVENTORY SYSTEM, SHIPPING AND RECEIVING SYSTEM.

**Problem:** Equipment breakdowns.
**Solution:** SCHEDULED MAINTENANCE SYSTEM with Checklist, and a REPAIR REQUEST SYSTEM which allows employees to report any equipment problems before they completely break down.

**Problem:** Rush jobs putting pressure on the production systems.
**Solution:** All of the systems previously mentioned; and having a DAILY PRINTED SCHEDULE for each work center. Rush jobs should be itentified by an asterisk, noting the first job that each person completes on their daily schedule. The rest of the schedule MUST BE COMPLETED and marked as completed before end of day or shift, unless management overrides. Each production employee is to turn in their Time Sheet and their COMPLETED schedule at end of day or shift. These will be reviewed systematically by management.

Eli Goldratt, in his 1980s book *The Goal* wrote, "The basis of TOC (Theory of Constraint) is, in every production process there are *bottlenecks* or *constraints* that determine the *throughput* of a factory or operation. Eliminating these constraints will greatly improve throughput."

I believe *some* constraints are not as obvious as the *bottlenecks* described by Goldratt. Many of the problems that cause chaos or slowdowns in production, which I have mentioned in this chapter, and over and over in this book, can *also* be considered bottlenecks— or what I call *system-busting events*. These can be easily fixed without adding more labor, purchasing new equipment, or—as in one of Goldratt's stories—taking out old equipment from storage to open a bottleneck in production.

# CHAPTER 15
# INTRODUCTION TO SYSTEM100™

I DESIGNED SYSTEM100™—a Business Process Management browser-based software—to download and automate the Operations Manual we had developed to organize and turnkey our company.

About the seventh year of building our Operations Manual, the company was running well, whether I was there or not, and I was completely out of debt. I could have semi-retired at a young age and gone fishing or golfing, but I felt there was something missing. What I was compelled to do was to take these systems and ideas I had discovered to the next level and make them public.

SYSTEM100™ is that next level. It serves as our company's "brain trust" and gives our employees direct access to the documents in our Operations Manual and many other automated systems, allowing them to do their jobs well, without micro-management.

SYSTEM100™ is a great tool to transform a company into a powerful, well-oiled machine. It provides a place to download the systems an owner has been carrying around in his head, into its database. We are constantly finding new ways of using SYSTEM100™ to automate the way we do business, and it is continually being reviewed and improved by many users from different types of organizations.

With SYSTEM100™, and using its Operations Manual as a guide, an organization would not have to spend 7-10 years building its own Manual from the ground up. We have already done the ground work. SYSTEM100™ will rapidly accelerate that process of systemizing and turnkeying your company.

Before I made the decision to design and develop SYSTEM100™ I scoured the business world for a solution like the one I had envisioned, hoping to save myself the time and money I knew it would take to develop it. Trust me, if I could have found it on the market at that time, I would have bought it without thinking twice.

If SYSTEM100™ software—which includes an Operations Manual—had been available to me from another source, when I first set out on the mission to turnkey my company, I would have thought I'd inherited a great fortune. I now know the power of good systems!

For more information on
**SYSTEM100™ SOFTWARE**
RECIPIENT OF THE INTERTECH TECHNOLOGY AWARD
www.System100.com

Ebiz Products
Ask@EbizProducts.com

# CHAPTER 16
## ENCOUNTERING OPPOSITION

WHEN YOU START BUILDING AND IMPLEMENTING systems, you can plan on opposition. This is where leadership comes into play. *Systems work! It's not theory, but fact!* If you want to systemize and turnkey your organization, be ready to take a stand. And also be ready to be humbled.

### They Say, "Systems Will Never Work"

One day in the early years of building our systems, my son Paul came into my office and said, "Dad, why do you take so much grief from Bob, our graphics manager? Bob enjoys doing everything he can to find fault and problems with the systems you are trying to build. He is mocking and laughing at you behind your back, and saying these systems will never work."

I said, "Paul, it's okay, Bob is *helping* me."

Paul asked, "What do you mean?"

I said, "Although Bob is sometimes a pain in my side, and I would love to show him the door, he does find the holes and gaps in the system. Paul, imagine a system where Bob couldn't find any holes. What would we have?"

"A great system!" Paul replied.

I said, "*That* is exactly what we're trying to build—and we will build it!"

### Monkey Business

I'm no psychiatrist, but there are people in this world who seem to like a little chaos—some, *a lot* of chaos. I've met them, observed them and, yes, even confronted them. My sense of it is, they feel safe somehow, because they can hide in the confusion. They can point fingers and blame others in a chaotic organization with poorly designed systems. And who could prove otherwise? When a manager's or owner's attention is diverted away, due to chaos and lack of systems, a lot of hiding the truth and monkey business goes on.

Have you ever seen the gorillas on TV's *Animal Planet* running around kicking up dust and shaking the branches? It's quite a spectacle, and looks like some important activity is going on there. All the other gorillas are very impressed with the commotion, but it's all smoke and mirrors, or as we say down South, "just a big ol' show for the folks." In a company that is chaotic, some people act the same way—looking busy, desk overflowing with papers, running to and fro, but actually just kicking up dust. Some management may be impressed with the bustle of such an employee. When they pass by them, they hear things like, "Whew, rough day, I'm worn out," or those famous words, "I need more help!" These kinds of folk do not care for a structured system, because they will be exposed by it, and you will encounter their opposition.

Other people feel insecure about their abilities, and the system is asking questions they've never before had to answer. Their pride, talent and organizational abilities are being challenged.

Some people have come from companies with poorly designed systems where they were *believed* to be very talented, organized, and knowledgeable—they may even have been celebrated at their former employment. You see, some people may see themselves as a *nine* on a scale of one to ten, but when they encounter a well-structured system that actually measures their efficiency, they may be exposed as a much lower number. This person doesn't like a well-structured system, and you'll meet with opposition. Are you ready for the challenge? Will you stand?

*All truth passes through three stages. First, it is ridiculed.*
*Second, it is violently opposed.*
*Third, it is accepted as being self-evident.*
Arthur Schopenhauer

## No "Sacred Cows"

Some years ago we had a very skilled department manager in our company, whom I thought at the time we couldn't do without. I'll call him "John." He was highly technical and a very dependable employee; however, the system was showing he had some work habits that needed serious improvement. I had a meeting with John and expressed my concerns. He said he would work on it, but after a few months, the system showed that John's bad habits had not changed. He was still not adhering to the system. I had to make a very difficult decision at that time. Do I tell others in our company they have to adhere to the system, but because I may be thinking of John as some kind of "sacred cow"—an employee that I'm afraid to lose—I will continue to make an exception for John's behavior? If I did that, I might as well stop right now and throw the years of building systems, that were transforming us into a well-organized company, right out the window.

By that time, I had invested eight years into building our systems and I couldn't look our employees in the eyes and tell them we could not do without John. The rubber was about to meet the road. The systems were either what I claimed they were, or they were not. I met with John and again told him he was either going to adhere to the system, or he would have to leave.

He said, "Well, to tell you the truth, I really don't like these systems."

I said, "John, thank you for telling me the truth. I know you don't, but I am sold on them, because I have seen the benefit for our customers, employees and myself by having them."

We parted friends and our company saw an immediate improvement in production and in other areas. We didn't miss a step. As a manager, John was hindering our progress. This decision sent a message to all of our employees, that I would not yield to anyone's not adhering to the system, and we would stay the course on continual improvement.

You can expect certain employees coming to your office complaining about having to adhere to the system; saying they are "tired of being called out" for every mistake. You will need to instruct them that it's not you, nor their supervisor, who are pointing out their mistakes—it's "the system" that is pointing them out. You will also need to remind them they should be glad their mistakes are being found, because the system also demands that we show them how to correct them.

Yes, there will be opposition—but if our goal is one of excellence, we must take a stand!

*Cast out the scoffer and contention will leave—*
*yes, strife and reproach will cease.*
Solomon the Wise

# CHAPTER 17
## ARE YOU ON THE RUN?

I LEARNED A LOT ABOUT CHICKENS when I was a boy. After my mother died suddenly, I went to live with my Aunt Ducy in Pearl River, Louisiana. I was nine years old, and the fact that my aunt raised chickens, along with other small farm animals, helped to keep my mind off more serious things. Chickens can be very funny, but when Aunt Ducy's chickens got to a certain age it was time to get them ready for the freezer. *My* job was to catch the chicken—*that* was funny—and hand it to Aunt Ducy. Then I'd stand off about ten feet, while she would calmly lay the chicken's head on a stump, raise her little hatchet, and WHACK! *Not* so funny! But so goes farm life! When a chicken loses its head it will often run around in circles for a time, until it runs out of steam and keels over . . .

*Reminds me of some businesses I've observed!*

A company without a good head for systems is apt to flail around for a while, but it will eventually collapse. In the same way, if a leader fails to download the systems he keeps in his head—should he leave the business for any reason—the systems go with him and the business is in danger of collapsing. This is why many *second-generation* businesses fail.

Earlier, we talked about how you need to *download,* so all that information you carry around in your head is readily available to your staff, and they don't feel the need to corner you every time you walk through your company or a department. Have you grown tired of having one staff member after another pull you aside to ask you the same questions for the umpteenth time?

Have you given your staff a manual where they can find the answers for themselves? No? Okay, so you have become "Mama," and they will continue to pull at you like a small child tugging on its mother's skirt while she has both hands in the sink, the phone ringing, and another child crying for attention.

"Hey Bob! You think you could get me a . . ."

"Hey Bob! My uncle is visiting. I need time off . . ."

"Hey Bob! Can you have this light fixed . . ."

"Hey Bob! Would you talk to so and so about . . ."

This gets old! The reason owners and managers get burned out is because they have no systems to handle all these questions and pressures. It's not very hard then to understand why some of them hide out, sneak in and out of the building, close their doors to employees and problems. No surprise they have glassy, far away looks in their eyes. Some even throw tantrums and attend "Happy Hour" all too frequently.

In his book, *The E Myth*, Mr. Gerber wrote:

*YOU are the problem*

*YOU have always been the problem*

*YOU will always be the problem*

*—until YOU change*

I can tell you, I thought long and *hard* about that!

*Denial ain't just a river in Egypt.*
Mark Twain

## Great Expectations

You should not expect your employees to do the job the way *you* think they should, unless you have provided them the necessary tools and the time in which to complete it.

In other words, if your employees come running up to you every time you walk through the various departments to ask you every question under the sun, then you haven't given them the tools or the systems to do their job.

However, once you've given them the tools to do their job, they should be *expected* to use them.

## The Right Tools

A well-known speaker on continual improvement in business used a very effective demonstration with CEO's and managers of some very large corporations. This involved bringing a group of them to the front of the room and giving each one a box of black and white marbles all mixed together. He would tell them their assignment was to separate the white marbles from the black marbles, and he gave them one minute in which to do it. He assured them it could be done in one minute or less, because *he had done it himself.* He would then start the timer and the CEO's and managers would begin frantically separating the marbles into different boxes, while everyone else was laughing and cheering them on.

After one minute the speaker would say *stop*! Everyone would look around to see if the others had completed the separation and, of course, no one had.

Then the speaker would ask, "Why couldn't *you* complete the job? You expect your employees to complete jobs in a set amount of time, and when they don't you get upset. In many cases, you haven't timed the job to see how long it actually takes, or if it can be done consistently in a given amount of time. You don't supply them with the right tools or systems to do the job in the time allotted." The speaker would then add, "I gave you a simple task and *you* couldn't do it in the time allotted. The reason you couldn't—I didn't give you the TOOL."

At that point, from under a table, the speaker would pull another box with holes drilled in it. He would start the clock and pour the box of mixed black and white marbles into the box with the holes. Then he'd shake it around, and only the black marbles would fall through. No one had noticed the white marbles were slightly larger—too large to fall through the holes—and they remained in the box. The speaker completed the job of separating the marbles in about thirty seconds.

The moral of this story?

Give your employees the right tools and systems,
and they will consistently complete a task
to your specifications—and on time!

*We shall not fail or falter; we shall not weaken or tire.*
*Give us the tools and we will finish the job.*
Sir Winston Churchill

# CHAPTER 18
## THE LAND OF CHAOS

DON'T GO BACK!—to hiding from the truth, back to sweeping things under the rug, back to not fixing problems—back to "The Land of Chaos."

In the movie, *The Ten Commandments*—after Israel endured 400 years of slavery in Egypt—Moses (with no small help from God) was able to lead his people to freedom. However, after coming into some hardships and inconvenience, the Israelites began to grumble. They told Moses they were better off back in Egypt. Amazing! In a very short time, they had forgotten the cruel beatings, working in the mud pits, the back-breaking labor, moving tons of stone to build Pharaoh's tomb, all with no compensation.

You see, the Israelites had grown accustomed to the chaos and humiliating situation, even though they had been assured they were the people of promise. They even threatened to stone Moses for leading them out of bondage. Hmmm! But Moses persevered, and year-after-year he led the people toward the Promised Land. He faced the opposition and refused to turn back, because his eyes were set on the vision—the bigger picture. He knew where he was going and how great it would be for everyone when they finally got there. Moses was a true leader.

Yes, it can be really discouraging in the face of opposition, but a goal of totally systemizing your company only works if your commitment to it, as the leader, remains firm.

If you will lead, you will find those people who will follow you on your mission to becoming a world-class organization.

Good systems tend to expose lazy or incompetent employees, but they also expose the *good* ones. And isn't that what you want? I have found that good employees love a good system—while the others will often see your systematic way of organizing as "too rigid."

People who balk at systems will tell you they prefer a "relaxed, family-type" atmosphere. I call it a "loosy-goosy, shoot-from-the-hip, let-the-good-times-roll, as-long-as-it's-not-my-money-and-I'm-getting-paid-I'm-happy" atmosphere. Here is what they are really saying: "I want an atmosphere that doesn't require stewardship or accountability. I want an atmosphere where I can make all the personal phone calls I want—visit or gossip with everyone in the building when I want—play on the Internet when I want—take as many smoke breaks as I want—take my cat to the vet when I want—work the hours I want—and complain about everything under the sun, including the boss, when I want." These will also complain at holiday time when they don't get the bonus they want.

Go figure!

If you, as an employer, won't stand up to this type of opposition and intimidation, then I can tell you right now, you are wasting your time reading this book. You don't have what it takes! The only thing you *may* have left is a prayer.

Building a great organization—notice *organization* is the key word here—takes real commitment. It takes leadership and your willingness to lead when people are murmuring and wanting you to return to, or worse, remain the Land of Chaos.

But, if you turn your face into the winds of opposition, stay the course and journey on, you will reach the land of peace and prosperity—*joy* even. The rewards will be priceless!

*If you faint in the day of adversity, your strength is small.*
Solomon the Wise

## The Pay-Off

The truth of the matter is, building systems can be tedious work. Even after more than twelve years of building a great system, due to those *unpredictable events*, there can still be a few tough days, but they get farther and farther apart. To encourage our employees through such days, I remind them there are so many things going *right* at our company, we can only be thankful!

Several years ago, one of our front office employees voiced his concern, that since it was so quiet in the building, we must be having a slow month. I was able to assure him that we were actually having a very good month, and that the quiet and peaceful atmosphere was only further proof that our systems were really working.

## Confirmation—Don't Go Back!

As I was working on this book after hours at my office, I received a phone call from a former employee (I will call him Thomas) who had recently resigned to take a position at another company. To my amazement the first thing he asked was, "Can you tell me why the companies around this town have no checklist system for catching mistakes; and no one seems to care about quality?" He went on for about five minutes telling me about the chaos in Production at his new job, and about his boss' temper tantrums.

I said, "Thomas, it's not that they really don't care about the chaos—I believe they just don't know what to do, or where to start."

He said, "I've been trying to tell them how we did it when I was working for your company, but no one listens!"

Now, why was this call important enough to tell you about it in this book? Thomas is a fine person and I really like him. We share a lot of the same beliefs, but I'd had some difficulty with him adhering to the system. Thomas would tell you now that he has come to appreciate the difference good systems makes. His call to me was another strong confirmation.

> *Once you have tasted and seen*
> *the power of good systems,*
> *you will never want to*
> *return to the Land of Chaos!*

# CHAPTER 19
# LEADERSHIP:
# THE BUCK STOPS HERE

## Leadership

Recently, a friend gave me a book by Dr. John C. Maxwell called *The 21 Most Powerful Minutes in a Leader's Day,* in which he writes, "To go to the highest level you have to develop leaders—then you should develop leaders of leaders. Many leaders want to make followers, but at that rate you will only add to your organization one person at a time. But leaders who develop leaders multiply their growth, because for every leader they develop, they also receive all of that leader's followers."

Dr. Maxwell's book also says to, "Hire the best staff you can find, develop them as much as you can, and hand off everything you possibly can to them."

I agree with this premise for the most part. However, I am firmly convinced, to pass your vision on to someone effectively, it must be in *written* form. Also, a good system insures that the leader you are developing will have a greater chance at success. Your system is a powerful tool to give to this leader. As I mentioned earlier, the power of a system is—*you don't have to start over every time you replace one leader with another.*

Yes, I suppose you could hire a leader to set up the whole system, and go on your merry way, but I believe that's when it turns into *their* vision, and not yours. Later, if that leader decides to leave, you wouldn't know where he began or where he left off. You'd have to find another leader, throw him into the last leader's position, and tell him to swim. If he asked *how* and *where*, you could say, "You are a leader—figure it out!"

I tend to look for people who are smarter and more talented than me. When I interview people, I tell every one of them I am looking for a *leader*, not just an employee to fill a position. Then we provide them with the best tools we can afford.

## The Star of the Show is Not Always the Most Talented

Let me take you back to my old rock 'n' roll days, when I was a lead singer and bandleader. I always hired musicians who could also sing, as I wanted the best singers I could find. I had everyone in my band singing lead at some point in our show. I often had people tell me, "Philip, your bass player (or other band member) sings better than you do!" I wasn't intimidated by better singers, I learned from them, and it only made the *Philip Paul & Patrol Show* all the better. I had people who thought I was "great" and some who thought I stunk. But, so what! Not everyone was going to like me or my singing. There is probably no singer on the planet who ever took to the stage, where everyone was a fan. Again, what's important is the end product for the customer.

To become a great organization, you are wise to surround yourself with, and *appreciate*, other talented people.

*I not only use all the brains I have, but all I can borrow.*
Woodrow Wilson

*Iron sharpens iron; So one man sharpens another.*
King Solomon

## The Buck Stops Here

President Harry S. Truman kept a sign on his desk in the White House that read, THE BUCK STOPS HERE. In his farewell address to the American people, given in January 1953, President Truman referred to this sign by saying, "The President—whoever he is—has to decide. He can't pass the buck to anybody. No one else can do the deciding for him. That's *his* job!"

You must be willing to accept the truth about a situation and deal with it. You are responsible for *all* the decisions made in your company—even the ones made by your managers and employees.

In our software, SYSTEM100™, there is a button that says, THE BUCK STOPS HERE. All employees at our company have access to the program and they can click on that button, which produces a window with a comment field. There, employees can type in any serious problem(s) they are having and it is emailed directly to my home. This is *not* a system for submitting suggestions of improvements.

This particular system serves a very important function and has only been used a few times. Its purpose is to allow an employee to report mistreatment or dishonesty on the part of managers or co-workers, where the person reporting is afraid of retaliation. When someone uses this system I will very discreetly meet with them and assure them the information they sent me is between me and them. If they will not allow me to use this information to improve the situation, then I tell them it's *useless* information. However, I believe communication is key in all good systems, and if an employee *does* want to resolve the issue, all parties should then be brought together and this information put out on the table for each to give their side of the story.

I have found, when you bring people together in the same room, to discuss serious accusations or common issues, stories tend to be revised. I want my employees to know they can tell me the truth, and feel safe telling their manager or supervisor the truth, without being mistreated or alienated for speaking out.

The only way you can truly fix a problem or make good decisions is to determine the real truth of the matter. THE BUCK STOPS HERE SYSTEM is NOT used to spy on anyone or to play one person against another. But as the leader, you need to understand you are ultimately responsible for the well-being of your employees while they are at work.

If a manager or supervisor is intimidating your employees, causing them not to speak the truth or to hide problems from you, then you can only go so far in improving your organization.

THE BUCK STOPS HERE SYSTEM also sends a strong message to your managers and supervisors—they are not *better* than others in the organization, but have a leadership position. As leaders, they will be held to a higher standard, and held accountable for any decision not to improve the system by ignoring or squashing the truth. Some managers don't want to hear the truth, because when they *know* the truth, they also know they have to deal with it—and, quite frankly, some just don't want to deal with real issues.

Remember, *their* decisions are your decisions, and as I said before, THE BUCK STOPS HERE SYSTEM has rarely been used, but it serves as a strong deterrent to intimidation and dishonesty in your business.

*It is not good to show partiality in judgment.*
Solomon

# CHAPTER 20
# TQM AND ISO

## TQM

Total Quality Management is a system of continual improvement in every phase of a business. It is a process by which every person in a business—from the highest in management to the grounds keeper—is part of *learning* the system, *operating and using* the system, and *improving* the system.

A system of continual improvement will allow your company to achieve a high standard in service and production—not only improving service and production, but actually improving itself. In other words, this positive feedback loop guarantees that, as service and production improve, the system of improvement *also* improves.

### A Deming Story

Earlier, I mentioned W. Edwards Deming, the namesake of the Deming Application Prize for quality. He was another source from which I learned about the importance of good systems and how they work.

W. Edwards Deming was an American whose ideas of continual improvement and quality management were rejected by American auto and other manufacturers until about 1980. America, at one time, controlled most of world's automobile manufacturing market and didn't see the need for vast improvement. At the end of World War II, Dr. Deming went to Japan to conduct a census for the U. S. Government as part of the rebuilding of Japan. While in Japan, the Union of Japanese Scientists and Engineers (JUSE) had heard of Dr.

Deming's quality theories and invited him to give a lecture. The Japanese were so inspired by his theories of quality and continual improvement, some of the largest manufacturers, such as Toyota and other companies, implemented his ideas into their manufacturing.

As you may know, some Japanese companies were starting from the ground up after the devastation of World War II. In the 1950s, a product labeled "Made in Japan" was thought to be junk. I remember as a kid hearing people laugh about and mocking Japanese products, but getting on into the 1960s and 1970s we all stopped laughing. In fact, American businesses became very fearful of Japanese products, because the little Toyota, bought as a "second car," was lasting ten years with hardly any maintenance, and the big American family car was falling apart and constantly in need of repair.

Well, you can guess what happened next. Americans bought more and more Japanese cars and Japan started taking a larger share of the market. Through the Continual Improvement System, Japanese cars became more and more reliable and the process used to build their cars became more and more efficient. All defective parts were inspected, then marked for improvement, along with every process to build, service and market them.

Today the *Deming Application Prize* is the highest award you can receive in Japan for quality. After America lost much of the world market, and Dr. Deming was in his eighties, we began to wake up.

### Dr. Deming Helps Ford

One of the first, large American corporations to seek Dr. Deming's help, was Ford Motors. Ford executive persuaded them to visit their headquarters in Dearborn, Michigan, in February, 1981. The company's sales were falling, and Ford was losing hundreds of millions of dollars.

Ford management was expecting a presentation with a bag of tricks for an instant fix—on how to improve quality in order to turn the company around. Instead, Dr. Deming insisted on questioning the company's culture and management philosophy. He explained to them that eighty-five percent of their quality problems were the result of management errors. This made for lots of bruised egos.

In many of Dr. Deming's seminars and lectures at Ford, he emphasized that *quality starts at the top*, and executives are not to be treated as if they are more important than those working the assembly line. Leaders should have a servant's heart and encourage their workers to use their minds, as well as their hands, on the job.

Dr. Deming sent a clear message to upper management, that quality is everyone's business, and everyone has a part in the system of continual improvement. He assured them that quality is a way of thinking, and it takes commitment.

Adopting Dr. Deming's ideas, Ford's success grew along with the quality of their automobiles.

Again, it was fear that motivated Ford and other companies to give Americans the quality they deserved, and only because they were losing business to the Japanese. I never want to lose business due to poor quality and service for lack of continually improving. We ought to thank the Japanese for their dedication to quality—otherwise, we still might be driving piles of junk.

I have owned three Ford vans since the "Quality is Job One" marketing campaign started. Every one of them has been great. In fact, my 1990 Ford van was used as a delivery van and my personal transportation. We put 250,000 miles on it, then I gave it to my son who drove it another 50,000 miles before he sold it.

Thanks, Japan, for kicking us in the rear end—we have been the beneficiaries!

## ISO

You may or may not be familiar with ISO, the International Standards Organization, headquartered in Geneva, Switzerland. It is an organization composed of a group of national standards institutes from 157 countries.

Maybe you've seen their large banners on the sides of buildings—CERTIFIED ISO 9000, and didn't know what it meant. The 9000 stands for a type of quality certification.

ISO develops standards for quality control and other management control systems. It was set up to help companies standardize quality control systems, services and other business practices.

One effective policy used by ISO-certified companies is to buy parts and services only from companies that have strict quality controls, continual improvement systems, and who share the same goals and ideas for quality and service—usually another ISO-certified company. Let's say, for example, a company manufactures headlights and is a vendor for Toyota. Toyota not only insists on quality headlights, but also proof from the vendor that the headlights will be continually improved, along with the manufacturing process.

Now, imagine each part of Toyota's cars getting better each and every year. Every time a part of the car is found to be defective, they notify all personnel responsible for those defects, and come up with ideas to improve the quality system so it won't happen again. They are not looking to place blame. No, they want to *fix* the problem as a team. They are not interested in trying to cover up problems—they are interested in gaining market share by making a great car for the customer.

### Nintendo™ Inspector Pays a Visit

A few years ago, an inspector from Nintendo™ came to audit our company. He wanted assurance we had systems that would insure quality printing and service, because our printing would reflect on their product, and they demand quality. Since we had control systems required by ISO, and had been effectively using these quality systems and services, we were certified to print Nintendo™ products. Nintendo™ is ISO-certified and they require their products be printed by a company that shares their values and quality standards. We have had several ISO-certified companies visit our facility for inspections. We understand that through good systems we can compete at the highest levels. Today, business is becoming a global market and we must keep improving in order to compete on the world stage, as well as the local market. Some are intimidated by ISO because of its complexities. Let me share a story with you...

### ISO For Dummies

About twelve years ago, when I started my mission to systemize my company, I read an article about ISO and became curious.

I called a consulting firm that implements ISO standards in order for companies to become certified. I didn't really know what ISO was all about, but an article I read about ISO, and the system of continual improvement, sounded like something I ought to look into. I got someone on the phone at this firm and began questioning him about ISO. I understood little of what he was saying, but—so as not to sound totally ignorant—I asked him to send me the ISO manual and other literature we had discussed.

"How many employees do you have?" he asked.

"Five, I said, "including myself."

There was a long pause on the other end of the phone and then he said, "No, you don't understand, Mr. Beyer, this is for *large* companies! The cost can be up to a quarter of a million dollars to implement. You will need to hire a consultant to help you implement and understand these systems. They have people to write policies and procedures for you."

Not wanting to be talked out of it, I told him I planned on *being* a large company one day, and I needed to get started right away understanding ISO systems. He sent me the manual. Well, he was right! When I received the manual and literature, I opened them and started reading. It didn't make much sense, at that point. Terms like "Non-Conforming Processes," and others they used, were hard for me to understand. I picked up a word or two and a couple of ideas, but not very much.

I continued to build systems on my own. When you are managing a business, you know what needs to be fixed and you don't need ISO or anyone else to tell you that, because it's already happening to you. After a few years of building systems, I picked up the ISO manual again and I was amazed that I understood a lot more than I had before. After a few more years, I opened it again and I had *more* understanding. I realized I was doing a lot of the same things, but felt that *our* methods were easier to understand. Eventually, the entire ISO manual made sense.

You remember earlier I was talking about Nintendo™ being ISO-Certified, and the inspector auditing our systems. Well, as he was leaving he turned to me and said, "You have one of the most organized and cleanest printing plants I have ever audited. In fact, I believe you could pass and be ISO-certified, if you wanted to." I was on cloud nine. It was one of those proud moments at our company.

## ISO—Not Just a Gimmick

A friend shared with me how the president of a very large commercial printing company in California, where she sold printing, had said to her that ISO was just a gimmick used as a marketing tool. This president said he didn't need systems—he just needed good people. My friend told me two out of three jobs she shipped to her customers had something wrong with them. But when she complained to the production manager, he would throw a tantrum and try to intimidate her to keep the matter quiet. One day she reported his behavior to the president and he informed her the reason she was hired was to smooth things over with customers. He also implied that, production problems were the "everyday norm" in printing.

I say, chaos is *not* normal!

My friend was really being told she was hired to make excuses (lie) for the company. Truth is, they were too lazy and prideful to fix their problems by incorporating good systems.

These types of leaders would have you believe ISO or any proven quality or service system is a gimmick. Apparently, the president of that California company believes it is easier to hire sales people to make excuses—and implement a "system of apology"—than to build a system that eliminates errors and internal chaos. Apparently, it's not about their customers and employees—it's all about *them*!

Let me assure you, the ISO system and our system are not fads, nor gimmicks. They work! But you must be committed to using them.

*The quality of a person's life is in direct proportion to their commitment to excellence, regardless of their chosen field of endeavor.*
Vince Lombardi

# CHAPTER 21
## CLOSING THE CIRCLE

IN THE BEGINNING OF THIS BOOK I shared a vision I had of circles that, to me, represented systems intersecting and interacting with each other. I hope, by now, you understand the importance of systems, and that you are not put off by what may seem my *overuse* of the word SYSTEM.

I actually had one reader comment that the book you are reading mentioned "systems" way too much. I didn't know how to respond to his comment, as I was sure the title of the book made the contents a dead give-away. Organizing your business permanently—not just a quick fix—is all *about* SYSTEMS!

When you build and complete all the needed systems in your organization so that they work together in concert—with no gaps— you have created a turnkey operation.

Seemingly complex things are not really so hard to understand or build when you break them down into small steps. The most complex part of creating your systems will be bringing two or more systems together. Each system in your organization affects every other system.

You, the leader, must bring your people together as a team to find and fix the holes or gaps, so the interacting systems will not affect each other in a negative way. You must also learn to be patient, but persistent, in the creation of your systems for your turnkey operation, which will be documented in the OPERATIONS MANUAL.

As you can see, building these systems will not happen overnight. It's a commitment, but it's worth it!

## Let's Recap and Close the "Circle" of this Book

As you fix the big gaps and holes in your systems, you gain more time and profit, allowing you to fix and tweak even *smaller* ones, where you gain even *more* time and profit.

Around and around you go, until you've created a business that will run like a super-clean, well-oiled machine, every single day from now until the end of time—whether you are there or not!

YOU NOW OWN A BUSINESS!

YOU NO LONGER HAVE JUST A JOB.

Oh, by the way, remember "Cranky" in Chapter 1?

*Now here's "The Rest of the Story"...*

Cranky no longer has to open his business every morning, since he systemized his operation. In fact, Cranky doesn't have to come to the office but several hours a week, unless he just wants to. He doesn't have "just a job" there anymore. He now OWNS a business, and his eyes and ears are the very systems he has implemented.

He now receives financial and other reports via email to his mobile phone—on his house boat. He can also go on the Internet and log into his company Intranet—e.g., SYSTEM100™—and communicate with anyone in his company, at any time of the day or night.

His is now a turnkey business which is franchise-ready. If he decided to sell, it is now worth much more than before he systemized.

Remember how Cranky's employees arrived at different times? Well, now they ALL arrive to work on time, because there is an ABSENT/TARDY SYSTEM in place, complete with:

1. A POLICY stating the start and end-of-shift times for each department.

2. An on-line system—e.g., if Worker Sue arrives late she is to submit an ABSENT/TARDY REPORT, with her name, the total time she is late, and the reason. Then she clicks "submit." This takes about fifteen seconds.

**3.** A DAILY ROUTINE CHECKLIST, which prompts Worker Sue and other employees to submit an ABSENT/TARDY REPORT whenever they arrive late. This avoids the excuse, "I forgot."

**4.** A COMPUTERIZED TIME CLOCK SYSTEM on which she clocks in and then out at the end of the day, at which time she prints out her own TIME SHEET and turns it in with her DAILY ROUTINE CHECKLIST to a designated location.

**5.** A follow-up system for the ABSENT/TARDY REPORT, whereby, everyone's TIME SHEET, along with their DAILY ROUTINE CHECKLIST, is reviewed by Bookkeeper Mary who, by the way, is now also the Human Resources Supervisor.

As you can see, with just an ABSENT/TARDY SYSTEM properly implemented—no gaps—Cranky brought a lot of order to his business. Yes, this took time, but Cranky would say, "Great systems work!" But there's much more!

The next part of the Cranky story told how Bookkeeper Mary tended to send Worker Sue to the bank, due to the fact that Bookkeeper Mary usually arrived late, and she didn't have a car. Since the ABSENT/TARDY SYSTEM was implemented, Bookkeeper Mary arrives on time. Going to the bank is on her DAILY ROUTINE CHECKLIST, and it is also a part of her JOB DESCRIPTION.

It seems she was able to get her car fixed, since she's no longer able to borrow Cranky's car, as he's out fishing on the lake. My guess is, she felt her job might be in jeopardy, since Cranky's business is no longer a loosey-goosey, let-the-good-times-roll operation.

Worker Sue is no longer interrupted to go to the bank, and the fact that she couldn't go on Tuesday doesn't even come into play. She is now able to do the work she was hired to perform, which is listed on her JOB DESCRIPTION and also on her DAILY ROUTINE CHECKLIST.

Bookkeeper Mary has now been trained to do payroll, and has a step-by-step PAYROLL PROCEDURE to help her if she forgets or misses a step. Now Worker Sue is no longer interrupted to do payroll, and Cranky should *never* have to do it again.

Productivity is up and Worker Sue is very happy. Worker Sue and all of the employees have been trained to use the REQUEST FOR

LEAVE SYSTEM, and when her dog Scooter has to go to Doggie Daycare she is required to give a week's notice using a REQUEST FOR LEAVE. Now if her request is approved, it should mean production is normal, her supervisor has been notified, and the leave date has been placed on the COMPANY CALENDAR so as not to be forgotten. Another worker will be able to take her place while she is absent.

Oh, by the way, Worker Sue now has her retired mother-in-law taking Scooter to Doggie Daycare.

Things are really running smoothly at Cranky's business.

CSR Jim is no longer required to take care of problems in production, as one of the workers has been trained on how to respond to, and report, problems. A CHAIN OF COMMAND POLICY has been written, and everyone trained on who-to-go-to, with what.

A PREVENTATIVE MAINTENANCE SYSTEM and a REPAIR REQUEST SYSTEM have been implemented so there are fewer equipment problems.

A QUALITY CONTROL SYSTEM has also been implemented in production, and errors are down to less than half of 1 percent. Wow!

CSR Jim can now concentrate on serving customers, and since the DATA ENTRY CHECKLIST for entering orders has been implemented, there are almost zero data entry errors. Other departments aren't constantly calling Customer Service trying to find missing information. All is quiet in Customer Service.

Salesman Bob is on Cloud 9, since all these systems have been implemented. His customers are no longer calling him, complaining about billing and production errors, or the status of an in-progress order. Quite frankly, his customers never knew what to expect before. And since the new SCHEDULING SYSTEM has been implemented, orders are on time, every time, for every customer. Salesman Bob is now able to take care of customer relationships and has time to call on new prospects.

Salesman Bob's customers are always complementing him about the neat appearance of the shop, since the 100 PERCENT SYSTEM OF CLEANLINESS has been installed. With the new AUTOMATIC MARKETING SYSTEM rolling, Salesman Bob has had three record months in sales.

You'll be happy to know, "Cranky" is no longer cranky! Last I heard, Cranky was writing a book.

*God is not the author of confusion.*
Paul of Tarsus

## Benefits of a Systemized and Turnkey Organization

- Market value of your company is substantially increased

- More time for your personal life

- Satisfied customers give free word-of-mouth promotions

- Vendors give free, positive word-of-mouth promotions

- More effective employees

- More peaceful work environment

- Fewer and more productive meetings

- Fewer and more effective managers

- Improves employee cooperation

- Quickly reveals employee work habits

- More profit with fewer mistakes

- Time and money saved by good housekeeping

- Employees take pride in clean and organized work areas

- Less customer turnover

- Less employee turnover

- Better service and more respect from vendors

- Attracts quality employees who attract other quality employees

- Production through-put is shortened with less exertion

- More time/resources to give back to your community

- More time to serve customers and address their problems

- Easier to manage

# CHAPTER 22
# A Little Lagniappe (extra)

My father, Henry T. Beyer, Jr., was from New Orleans, Louisiana, and I remember he liked to use the word *lagniappe* (pronounced lan-yap) when he was teaching us about going the extra mile for other people. It's a French/Creole term that means "a little extra," like a small gift given to someone. So, here's a little *lagniappe* for those with small or start-up businesses.

## The Information Age

Today we're living in what is called the "Information Age." I suggest you take advantage of the information, but don't get bogged down in it. I highly recommend you read trade publications about your industry or business, as these are a source of very valuable information. People in your industry are going through the same things you are—you can learn from them. There is no reason to re-invent the wheel, but by all means improve upon it.

Look for articles, cut them out, organize them, and give them to others in your company. For years I have been saving articles on sales, service, management, production, TQM, etc., and have used, and put into practice, the tips and information I've gleaned from these publications. I find now, many new articles are confirming what we have already implemented and believe to be good business practices.

As you hire new employees, give them access to these tips. We scan these tips and load them into System100™. Motivated employees appreciate them. So don't get frustrated when some don't take them as seriously as you think they should. The important thing is that YOU take them seriously, because the information from these articles and tips can be used to help you grow as a leader and as an organization.

## Embrace Technology

I strongly suggest if you are starting a business or organization, it is crucial you start by using the technology that is available to you at affordable prices. You should be using bookkeeping/accounting software such as QuickBooks. All types of software can be found on the Internet and can pay for itself—in some cases, in the first few months. In fact, most of the software I've purchased has paid for itself many times over.

If you are one of those companies that have been in business for a few or even many years, and are not using a computer for your bookkeeping and other operations, I recommend you look into these time-saving tools.

I know companies that have been in business for thirty years and have few or no computers for the operation of their business. The cost is lost time and information. That, I believe, is *self-inflicted blindness*—it's like using candles instead of light bulbs!

## Staying Encouraged

When you are a leader there will be times when no one is around to pat you on the back or to give you a word of encouragement. A leader does not have the option to hold a pity party.

*Your moods won't change things—only actions change things.* Take action over your moods by encouraging yourself with the reading of motivational books and trade journals; and by listening to tapes on successful leaders and organizations in and outside your industry.

I suggest reading materials that will help you gain wisdom and knowledge to help fix and eliminate problems in your business and your life.

We've all heard the phrase "garbage in, garbage out," and garbage is the thing that brings discouragement. Well-known motivational speaker, Zig Ziglar, calls it "Stinkin' Thinkin'."

Some people avoid solving problems by procrastinating. They work at things they find easier and more enjoyable, instead of the things they should. They let themselves be side-tracked by just about anything. When asked if they've completed a certain task, they're apt to tell you they just didn't have time or were too busy. Truth is, procrastinators tend to visit and interrupt others. They make personal phone calls, play on the Internet, make extra trips to the coffee pot, and usually talk way too much.

I believe procrastination is the number one reason people, businesses and organizations fail. Failure brings discouragement, and discouragement brings more failure. A person will not stop procrastinating, until they admit they do.

As I said in the beginning of this book, you have to face truth. How do I know about procrastinating? It was one of the struggles I had to overcome to move forward. I read books on the subject like one I recommended on page 143, *How to Gain an Extra Hour Each Day*. Do what ever it takes to stop procrastinating. I believe a DAILY ROUTINE CHECKLIST is a great tool to help eliminate this problem, by keeping you focused.

> *There are a million ways to lose a work day,*
> *but not even a single way to get one back.*
> Tom DeMarco and Timothy Lister

## Don't Act Great, Be Great

One of the most disturbing things I have observed in the business world is a company's practice of constantly looking for *new* business, while the customers they have aren't receiving anywhere near the service they deserve. They want *more* and *more* and when they get more, their customers get *less*.

Have you ever called a company to ask for technical help on a product they've sold you, or to ask a question about your bill, and you are put on hold for what seems eternity? When you finally get to talk to someone, they are often rude and evasive. Some companies out-source their Customer Service to a foreign country to save money. Then *you* have the frustration of explaining a technical problem to someone who has a difficult time understanding you, and you them. Yet, if you turn right around and call that same company's *Sales* line, they will answer almost immediately with a more receptive person. This is all the evidence you need to see where a company's priorities are. They put a high premium on sales, and not service.

How many times have you had telephone companies begging you to switch to their service, and once you sign up you can't even get them on the phone? And think of the TV commercials that promote a company's "greatness," and then you're disappointed to find they are *not* great—it was all just *great* promotion.

During the first ten years we were building our company's systems, I refused to put the emphasis on sales. I believe you should be a good steward of what you have and grow step-by-step.

Never sacrifice quality and service for a quick buck.

> *He who is greatest among you shall be your servant.*
> The Word

## The Worker is Worth His Wages

Paying higher wages for skilled employees can be a difficult decision for organizations and businesses, especially if you are a small operation. I've lost some very qualified applicants, because I feared I might not be able to afford them. I remember not hiring someone because he wanted a dollar-an-hour more than I was paying, or thought I could afford. He went to work for another company and became a star employee. I heard later through the grapevine, he did the work of two or three people.

Good employees pay for themselves!

When I bought my first large printing press, which was going to cost more than my house, I remember thinking, "How am I going to afford this press and a press operator to run it?" I made the trip to New Jersey to inspect and purchase the press. While I was there, I had the opportunity to spend time with the plant manager, who was answering my questions concerning the press.

He said, "Philip, I would like to give you some advice. When you hire an operator for this press, do not hire someone just because they will work for a few dollars less an hour. Look for a great operator and be ready to pay a top wage—they will earn every dime of it. In fact," he said, "They will make you money!" But I didn't listen because of fear, and immediately upon returning, looked for someone who would work for what I thought I could pay.

I hate to admit this, but that little lesson cost me more than I would like to state in this book. I finally learned that lesson although it was a slow process. Now, I can also make the statement with much experience under my belt: Great employees *do* earn their pay, and they *will* make you money. They will help you in your mission to build a great organization.

But remember, great employees do not replace a great system. You need *both* to develop a great company.

*It's not what you pay a man, but what he costs you that counts.*
Will Rogers

## Take Good Notes

Owners, managers and everyone looking for ways to fix problems and improve the organization should *always* keep a pen and paper handy to make notes as they get ideas, or notice things that need improvement. When I first started to systematize my business, I literally took thousands of notes and would transfer them into a to-do list on my computer.

It's our policy to come to meetings prepared with any notes and a fresh pad. As an owner, it's very frustrating to hold a meeting to discuss improving the company, and the very people who have been complaining about problems often show up without any written notes that might list their concerns or possible resolutions. Valuable time is wasted while they try to recall the details.

## Buy Cheap, Buy Twice

You have heard this before—but *listen* this time! When you buy poor quality product for your business, because it's cheap or you think you are getting a great bargain, it may end up costing you more and give you more headaches in the long run. Now, I'm not saying you shouldn't look for a bargain. Being a good negotiator and trying to control spending can mean the success or failure of a business. But being a tightwad can hurt your business.

Here's an example of what I'm talking about:

When I implemented my 100 PERCENT SYSTEM OF CLEANLINESS I purchased some cabinets made of heavy gauge steel. I also bought some of those thin steel cabinets you find at office supply chains and other discount stores. The thin cabinets are easily bent and, if you move them, the doors get warped and won't close properly. I have had to replace, or am in the process of replacing, every one of them. The heavy steel cabinets still look as good as the day I bought them, other than a few scratches. When we moved to our new facility we didn't have to take everything out of the cabinets, we just put them on a dolly with their contents.

Another example of this would be if you have a high traffic area and your carpet is constantly in need of cleaning. Why not consider tile? Yes, tile costs more, but if you buy the right kind of tile it can last a lifetime. It looks good and it is easily cleaned, unlike carpet. In the long run you save money and your business looks great.

## Pay Your Bills

When I started my company in 1988 I asked my brother Billy, a Louisiana business owner, if he had any advice he could share with me to help me succeed. To my surprise, he said, "Pay your bills!"

*Caution:* In your business you will have money flowing through your bank account, but it is not ALL your money. It belongs to your vendors and your employees—and it's meant to cover other expenses your business will have. If you start spending money already allocated, you will find yourself in deep trouble, and probably lose the business.

He was right! I have seen many businesses go out of business, not for lack of business, but because the owner over-spent on his personal life, rather than pay his company's bills.

During the first eight or nine months I was in business I didn't take a dime for myself. Even after that, I only lived on the profits. I made sure my employees and vendors were paid first. This has been very valuable to our business, and when we had to go through some tough times, our vendors were behind us all the way. They knew our word was good, and they extended the credit I needed to get us through and keep production rolling.

The SBA (Small Business Administration) Website says one of the reasons for business failure is personal use of business funds. You can't get any clearer than that!

*Do not say to your neighbor, "Go, and come back,*
*and tomorrow I will pay you," when you have it with you.*
Old Proverb

**Barter or Trade Organizations**

Barter or trade organizations are set up for small businesses to find new customers. There are several such organizations out there, like ITEX and Trade Bank. You become a member for a small start-up fee and they place your business name with all their members. If someone needs your product or service they use *trade dollars* to purchase them. Trade dollars are printed checks with the trade organization's name and information on them. You build up a trade bank account just like you would with real dollars. When you need a product, you call one of the members in the organization to get a price and, if you like the price, you purchase with your trade dollars.

There are a couple of things to be aware of:

• You pay sales tax just like you would with real money, unless you're exempt on certain items.

• You claim the sales in your accounting just like you would with any other sales.

• Some members of trade organizations mark their products up higher than normal if they know someone is using trade dollars as opposed to real dollars. This is not supposed to happen, as you can be ousted from the organization for this type of practice. But, from what I have seen, this policy is not strictly enforced.

Just like any other purchase you make, you need to be alert. "Let the buyer beware!" goes the old adage.

I have found that certain trade organizations may be stronger in one city than in another. Before you join, talk to some local members. They can tell you which is the strongest trade organization.

Some businesses are members of more than one organization. The strength of the trade organization depends upon the area director for a town or city.

Be careful not to over-spend or over-sell. If the cost to produce your product is high in hard dollars (real money), such as labor and materials, be very careful not to oversell. You can put your account "on hold," which means once you get your trade bank account to a certain figure you're comfortable with, you can stop selling.

A business, such as a hotel or radio station, benefits greatly with trade organization dollars, because it costs them little more to rent a hotel room that would otherwise be vacant, or air-time that would otherwise go unused.

When I first started out, I used trade dollars for office furniture, floor tile, and many other items. It also helped me establish friendships and network with other business people.

# CLOSING REMARKS

IF YOU HAVE FINISHED READING THIS BOOK, I want to thank you. I hope you have gleaned some ideas and information that will help you in your business and maybe even your life. Writing this book has been a milestone I will never forget.

As we were doing the final edits on this book two things became abundantly clear to me:

First, people are your greatest asset, and without them the gears of industry would not turn. If I have given the impression in this book that I believe systems can replace people, then I would like to set the record straight:

Systems do not eliminate the need for people—they are tools whereby fewer employees can produce more with less effort.

When a typesetting machine called the Linotype was invented at the turn of the 20th century, it was able to do the work of about six people who, at that time, set type by hand. But the machine *still* had to have an operator.

The Linotype was a *great* tool for mankind—but it didn't replace *all* type-setters. The type-setters that were replaced by the Linotype were compelled to pursue other important works that would benefit others.

The systems I value and explain in this book are tools to be a blessing to people. I hope this book has been a blessing to you.

Secondly, I might build a great turnkey business—one that has systems that would surpass any company on the globe, but a single Act of God could end it all. I pray every day for the blessing of God over my business and my life.

A GREAT system is a GREAT tool
to help people do a GREAT job!
Philip Paul Beyer

# PROFILE OF THE IDEAL OWNER OR EMPLOYEE

1. Honest with self and others

2. Eager to learn about their trade or position

3. Works well with others

4. Punctual

5. Good appearance and hygiene

6. Good work habits
   - Focuses on the task at hand
   - Not easily distracted or side-tracked
   - Takes pride in doing quality work
   - Keeps work area clean
   - Keeps work tools organized

7. Accepts constructive criticism

8. Does not blame others to cover his/her own shortcomings

9. Does not use offensive language

10. Not intimidated by change

11. Looks for ways to improve themselves and their work place

12. Shares knowledge to help others improve

13. Willing to go the extra mile

14. Does not condone wrong actions of supervisors or co-workers

15. Does not make improper advances to co-workers

16. Does not exploit stressful situations for personal gain

17. Respects supervisor's position in making tough decisions

# A View From My Window

A special lady who became my wife on July 16, 2005, wrote the following poem some years ago, and I was impressed enough to include it in this book, because it rang true for me as I worked to bring order to our business and our personal surroundings.

After a night behind curtain and shade
    I look out my window to see what God made
And the sight that I see makes me sad in my heart
    I think, "How much better, if all did their part"
'Cause the things in my view would take little to fix
    If each neighbor would bother to straighten and pickup
The rusty old pieces of this and of that
    Some towering eyesore, a discarded hat
Toys that a child has not treated with care
    Things taken out, not put back, lying there
A garden of tossed paper wrappers and such
    Making it right again wouldn't take much
If we each took a moment to think how our ways
    Might help out our neighbor and gladden his days
So all that we've worked for is easy to see
    Not hidden by refuse and piles of debris
God gave us so much in this beautiful place
    Mountains and forests, and smiles for each face
He gave us such wonders as music and light
    Colors and rainbows and eagles in flight
So, today I'll remember to do what I can
    To spread love around me, not paper and cans
If the world isn't all that God meant it to be
    Then I'll change what I can, beginning with me

—Susan Meredith Beyer, © 2001

Example

# Mission Statement

**W**e are in the business of assisting our customers in meeting their printing and print design needs. To this end, we are committed to providing the most consistent, high-quality and best customer service in our industry.

**T**o assure our customers of our promise of high quality and great customer service, our company employs only quality-minded, well-trained personnel. These assurances will be witnessed in every phase of our business with an emphasis on excellence, prompt service, courtesy, cleanliness, honesty, a genuine concern for our customers, and a QUALITY CONTROL SYSTEM that allows nothing to leave our facility that does not meet or exceed the expectations of our customers.

**O**ur quality and service control systems, work ethic, willingness to keep up with the latest industry innovations, and the offering of unique products will remain our hallmark and our vehicle toward new business.

**T**hrough these commitments, we build our futures, to the benefit of our company, our customers, ourselves, our children and our children's children for generations to come.

Example

# CODE OF ETHICS

We commit ourselves to a high standard of excellence, by adhering to a system of quality control checklists, during each phase of production.

We promise to accept only those projects or work we are able to produce, that will meet or exceed our customers' expectations.

We promise to maintain honesty and integrity in all dealings with customers and others.

We promise to treat each customer fairly and impartially.

We promise to respect the confidentiality of our customers' information, and protect their intellectual property.

We promise to charge fairly for all of our products and services— fair for the customer, our company, and our industry.

# SAMPLE ORGANIZATIONAL CHART

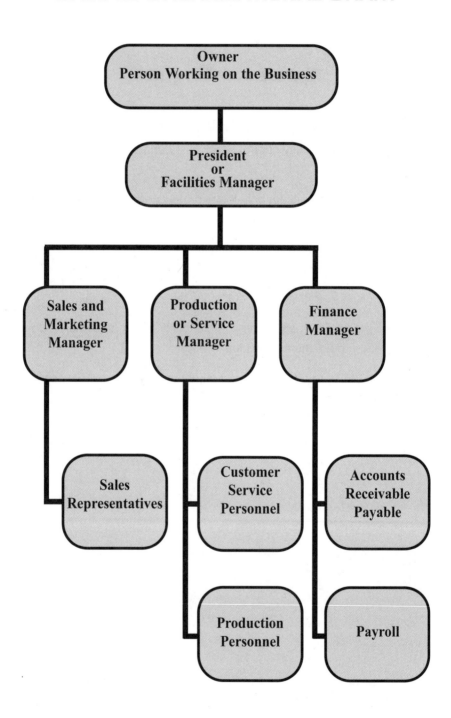

# Books We Recommend

*The Bible*
The New King James Version, © 1982 Thomas Nelson
This book has a lot to say about business.

*The E Myth*
by Michael Gerber. Harper Business, © 1986

*How to Gain an Extra Hour Every Day*
by Ray Josephs. Published by Thorsons, © 1992

*Automatic Marketing*
by Benjamin Hart, Profit Books, © 2006

*The Goal*
by Eliyahu M. Goldratt *and* Jeff Cox. North River Press, © 1984

*Taking the Mystery Out of TQM*
by Peter Capezio *and* Debra Morehouse. Career Press, © 1993

*The One Minute Manager*
by Kenneth Blanchard *and* Spencer Johnson. Berkeley Publishing
Company, © 1981

*Financial Peace*
by Dave Ramsey. Lampo Press, © 1992, 1995 and by the Penguin
Group, © 2003

*Delivering Knock Your Socks Off Service*
by Ron Zemke *and* Kristin Anderson. AMACOM, © 1993

*No Excuses Management*
by T.J. Rodgers. Currency, Book and Diskette edition, © 1993

*The 21 Most Powerful Minutes in a Leader's Day*
by Dr. John C. Maxwell. Thomas Nelson Publishers, © 2000

*Above "Reality"*
by Susan Meredith Beyer. © 2007
Not a business book, but I thought it good *business* to include it.

## WHAT OTHERS ARE SAYING

"Any business leader should read this book. It's an easy read and the 'systems' Philip discusses are very practical plans which, when implemented, will make any business successful. This book not only shows you what you need to do, but how to do it using actual examples as proof that it works. The key to all of it, no matter how simple, is that just having new systems in place won't work unless you use them!"

—Dave Ramsey, syndicated radio host and New York Times best selling author

"Hello. I just read *System Busters.*Thank you Philip! I heard about your book via an e-mail blast through Printing Industry of America. That e-mail was a true blessing. What I've learned from your book alone will change DSJ Printing and the life of my family and employees forever. We are a family owned and operated print shop. My Grandma and Grandpa started DSJ in 1953. My father is now president and we both work in customer service. Exactly what you described. He is 'Mama' to every employee here, myself included. He's constantly being tugged in every direction. To say the least, I felt it was becoming overwhelming for him. When you mentioned having implemented one system at a time. This piece of advice will take a huge load off both of our shoulders, by giving him more time to do his work and by helping me work on getting him into retirement. Your book is a serious eye opener. Thank you again. Please contact me ASAP regarding System100™. God Bless!"

—Jeffrey Vaughan, Jr., DSJ Printing, Santa Monica, CA

"This book is motivating and drives you to be a better business person. Since I started building our system, I have been able to identify the hidden, underlying problems that have continually set us back, and correct them. His Christian point of view is refreshing and reminds me of the importance of integrity in all regards. I have new hope and direction for my business. Six stars!"

—A. Parker, Parker Heating & Air, Smyrna, TN

"As a commercial printer in Omaha, Nebraska, in need of processes and systems, we searched for solutions to our continuing problems. We have eighteen employees and needed a way to communicate our vision of systemizing our business. We requested a copy of *System Buster* for each of our employees and passed them out as gifts. We are midway through our quest to systemizing our business and couldn't have done it without Philip Beyer's vision. Best regards."
—Garrett Anderson, Anderson Print Group, Omaha, NE

"This book helped me see the wisdom of systems for our business and ministry. Proverbs 8:12 says 'I, wisdom, dwell with prudence, and find out knowledge of witty inventions.' Philip's book helped me to find and improve upon the systems we use at The Gideons International. He invented a system to improve any system. Philip's work has opened my eyes to the benefits and blessings of well-planned organizational systems. He shares practical steps that can be universally applied to any business, association, ministry, even one's life. I intend to apply these concepts at every level from now on."
—Rodney Jones, The Gideons International, Nashville, TN

"I just read Philip Beyer's *System Buster* Book and thoroughly enjoyed seeing myself and our company in the book, repeatedly. What's more, I was thrilled to know that we're not that far off in our practices and there is a tried and proven system that's in place at Beyer, and it works."
—Jackie L. Griese, GGG Digital Graphics, Evansville, IN

"I am grateful that Mr. Beyer has allowed us all into his world, the world of 'hard core' business. Before reading and applying *System Buster* into my business, I would have to say that chaos was the word for the day. As we began to apply the principles inside the *System Buster.* We immediately saw a difference, the biggest of which was the recognition of how we lived from one "crisis" to the next. Everything has to have process, trackable process. I could

write for hours as a grateful business owner; grateful that Mr. Beyer has shared his 'found' insight with those of us who will be forever changed! Thank you, Thank you, Thank you!"
—Paul LaRue, Just Me! Music, Brentwood, TN

"Congratulations on your book and what it has meant to your business. My first read was very helpful. My operations manager is reading it now, then I'll take a second run-through, taking notes and building a "to do" list. Most important to me, *System Buster* gives me a series of models, which I am anxious to apply. Philip, thanks for the information and inspiration you offer in *System Buster.* It's full of wisdom! I'm going to get a couple more copies on order today. I'll keep mine at my side, give my operations manager one, and have the third available for other employees and my wife to read."
—Scott Fenneman, owner, Kwik Kopy Business Solutions, Evansville, IN

"Philip Beyer has developed a wonderful system of organization that is helpful to any business owner, manager or entrepreneur. His book, *System Buster*, helps people find more time, shows how to reduce workplace clutter, and gives a specific plan for increasing efficiency."
—Lisa Wysocky, motivational speaker and author of Success Within: How to Create the Greatest Moments of Your Life

"After reading the 'Buster' book, I agreed to a session on WebEx with Philip Beyer to test-drive his System100™ software in live, actual, operation. Never have I seen anything comparable to System100™ for a company! The System is a computerized method for the daily operation of Beyer Printing. Everything, and I do mean every last action in the commercial printing plant, appears to be covered. This is a checklist system to end all checklist systems! It all feeds into a computerized database written in an SQL language and every employee has access to a computer terminal for listings and forms. Then there's the piece de resistance: a sub-program called System Buster.

"When something happens that doesn't comport with the check lists, the *System Buster* detects the problem. It's immediately flagged for correction. I love the idea of System100™ and its checklists that assure personal accountability. Inventories are restricted. Delivery dates are kept. Invoices issue immediately. Plant cleanliness and equipment maintenance are assured. Every needed tool is immediately at hand. Everyone knows what's expected of him or her. Why haven't we done this before? Now, I've seen how a printing plant should be run. You deserve an award for showing me and the world what you can do when you really try. Small wonder that it took ten years to develop System100™. Every printing plant should have it!"

—Roger Dickeson, columnist, Printing Impressions magazine, Pasadena, CA

"I have just finished reading your book, *System Buster.* I was so sure this could be done. My husband and I purchased A-1 Printing almost five years ago. It has been in business since 1983. Along with the business, we acquired associates that have been here for a number of years. Anytime you suggest a new way of doing something, the walls go up, echoed by the words, 'We've tried that before and it didn't work.' Well, some of the things we have implemented have worked and with little flack. The biggest problem is nonconformance and accountability. I have struggled with this for the past year and started working on 'How to fix our problems.' I have learned from reading your book, that we are pretty much normal and just need to put more things in writing and hold people accountable. Thank you so much for the insight. Just reading your book has given me new hope and promise for a bright future."

—Barb Price, owner, A-1 Printing Inc., Bucyrus, OH

"I am in the process of reading your book *System Buster* and would like more information regarding your System100™ software. The book is wonderful. I find myself smiling and laughing out loud. I particularly appreciate your Christian business principles. Thank you!"

—Dan Goris, Ideal Printing Company, Grand Rapids MI

"Hey Philip! You might remember me. My name is Mark Hurt and I talked with you several times while I was in purchasing at World Media Group here in Indianapolis. I recently came across your book and started reading it, and could not put it down. I must say, I will practice this system effective immediately, and am excited of the end result. The best business book I have ever made good use with is *The E Myth,* which you are also aware of, and it appears your book will be in that category. I like the way you toss in verses from the greatest Book ever written (the Bible), as you don't see that in business books any longer. Well, to cut to the chase, I want my own copy and I want to buy a few extra for my brother's business as well as my dad's business, and I want to send some as Christmas gifts to many of my customers. Glad to see you are making a success at this."

—Mark Hurt, VIP Print Solutions, Indianapolis, IN

# INDEX

# Quotes

## ABOUT THE AUTHOR

PHILIP PAUL BEYER is founder and president of Beyer Printing, Inc. and Ebiz Products in Nashville, Tennessee.

Born and raised in Louisiana, Philip's interest in the art and craft of printing began at Tex Lyons' printing establishment in Baton Rouge. At fourteen, and already a budding entrepreneur, Philip was fascinated with his visits to the print shop and watching his brother Billy run presses. He marveled at the workings of the printing industry, and Tex soon offered him a job collating in the bindery department. Being able to work beside his brother, learning such exciting skills, and making fifty cents an hour was, for young Philip, the beginning of a deep appreciation of the printing trade—a life-long calling to a business that had revolutionized the world and changed the very course of history, with the advent of the Gutenberg Printing Press.

Philip entered into this creative industry during one of its most significant changes in half a century. Only a short forty years ago, printing was much different than it is today. It was a craft that found young people working as apprentices for years. Master printers were, and still are, a rare breed. Back then, a lot of printing was done on letter presses—slow by today's standards, but able to produce high quality results. The offset press was fast replacing the letter press, and the industry was changing rapidly.

While attending high school, Philip took a job as an apprentice at Kennedy Print Shop in Baton Rouge, where owner Carl Williamson, a Linotype operator, became one of Philip's most admired role models. During those years, he gained a wealth of knowledge about the trade that would build the foundation for his future.

After graduating from high school, Philip took courses very briefly at Louisiana State University until the lure of yet another powerful interest began to fill his thoughts. He had begun playing music and singing in school. In the late 1960s and early 1970s, music was just about every young man's fantasy, and Philip believed he had found his true calling. Leaving college, he worked all the harder as a printer to be able to afford and pursue his music interests. With this new incentive, he made it a point to learn everything he could about all facets of the printing trade—even keeping up with the latest industry trends. But, music had become his greatest passion.

By 1974, Philip's music was keeping him busy full-time and, although he would not enter the printing trade again for many years, his printing experience was put to good use in promoting his increasingly popular band, Papa Joe & Riverboat, later known as Philip Paul & Patrol. Looking at printing from the other side of the fence taught him lessons that would prove invaluable later as he related to his customers.

Eventually, however, the success of Philip's music was the very thing that began to take the greatest toll. He missed his family, and after twenty years on the road, with heavy performance and rehearsal schedules, Philip Paul hung up his microphone.

Philip Paul Beyer returned to a lifestyle he had longed for, instilled by Christian parents whose values and ideals were to become the solid basis for all his future endeavors. He had learned much from being a performer, bandleader and manager of a touring show—discipline, marketing and promotion. He learned how to take care of business, plan and keep schedules, meet payrolls, manage finances, and the importance of well-considered tools and equipment. He also learned about people, and most importantly, about integrity and relationships—where real success begins!

Still the entrepreneur, Philip remains dedicated to the highest quality products and service, and has found yet another professional passion, helping other entrepreneurs and business people reach their personal goals through strategic systematization of their operations.

Philip now speaks for special events and conferences, sharing his insights with business owners across America. He and his wife Susan make their home near Nashville, Tennessee.

To invite Philip Paul Beyer to speak at your next event, email ask@ebizproducts.com.